THE CIVIL RIGHTS MOVEMENT

BLACK POWER

THE CIVIL RIGHTS MOVEMENT

BLACK POWER

David Aretha

MORGAN REYNOLDS
PUBLISHING

Greensboro, North Carolina

The Civil Rights Movement: Black Power
Copyright © 2012 by Morgan Reynolds Publishing

Morgan Reynolds Publishing, Inc.
620 South Elm Street, Suite 387
Greensboro, NC 27406 USA

Library of Congress Cataloging-in-Publication Data

Aretha, David.
 Black power / by David Aretha.
     p. cm. -- (Civil rights movement)
 Includes bibliographical references and index.
 ISBN 978-1-59935-164-3 (alk. paper)
 1. Black power--United States--Juvenile literature. 2. Black Panther
Party--Juvenile literature. 3. African Americans--Civil
rights--History--20th century--Juvenile literature. 4. Civil rights
movements--United States--History--20th century--Juvenile literature. I.
Title.
 E185.615.A78 2012
 305.896'073--dc22

                                  2010046103

Printed in the United States of America
First Edition

Book Cover and interior designed by:
Ed Morgan, navyblue design studio
Greensboro, N.C.

TABLE OF CONTENTS

A *Black Power* pamphlet circulated by the Student
Nonviolent Coordinating Committee in August 1967

CHAPTER 1

A NEW KIND OF MOVEMENT

If you read certain history books, you would think that the civil rights movement ended on March 25, 1965, in Montgomery, Alabama.

Certainly it was a milestone day—the pinnacle of the nonviolent movement's decade-long campaign for equal rights. For three months, African Americans in nearby Selma, Alabama, had endured beatings, cattle prods, tear gas, and a fatal shooting in their efforts to register to vote. Two marches from Selma to Montgomery were aborted by police, including the infamous "Bloody Sunday" march. But the third march, supported by President Lyndon Johnson—who had promised six days earlier on national television to end all voting injustices with a voting rights bill—proved triumphantly successful.

On March 25, some 25,000 civil rights supporters gathered in the state capital of Montgomery to hear the soaring eloquence of Dr. Martin Luther King Jr. "Selma, Alabama," King roared to the masses that day, "became a shining moment in the conscience of man. There never was a moment in American history more honorable and more inspiring than the pilgrimage of clergymen and laymen of every race and faith pouring into Selma to face danger at the side of its embattled Negroes." **9**

With the Civil Rights Act having passed in 1964 and a voting rights bill in the works, King and his followers had achieved their lofty goal—equality under the law. Activists could leave Montgomery feeling as if they had written the last page of the civil rights story.

It may have been the final page, but only of Volume I. Volume II of the African American freedom struggle—known as the Black Power movement—was just beginning to unfold.

Stokely Carmichael, chairman of the Student Nonviolent Coordinating Committee, speaks at the University of California at Berkeley in 1966. He introduced the phrase "Black Power" to the civil rights movement.

On March 25, just hours after King's rousing speech, an incident occurred that proved that race was still a burning issue. While leaving Montgomery, white activist Viola Liuzzo gave black teenager Leroy Moten a ride back to Selma in her Oldsmobile sedan. Ku Klux Klansmen (KKK), enraged by the sight of a black man with a white woman, shot into the car, fatally hitting Liuzzo in the face.

The very next day, Stokely Carmichael arrived in Klan-infested Lowndes County, which was adjacent to the county that Selma was in. Carmichael was still a member of the Student Nonviolent Coordinating Committee (SNCC), but his ambitions were considerably different than those of King. Tall and lanky, Carmichael had once accepted but now rejected nonviolence as a tactic. A veteran of sit-ins, Freedom Rides, and voter registration campaigns, Carmichael had been arrested more than twenty times. He had endured the Freedom Summer voter registration campaign in Mississippi in 1964, when whites beat, arrested, and killed activists while burning and blowing up various homes and buildings.

With all the anguish that he had experienced—and the insight he had gained as a student at Howard University in Washington, DC—Carmichael had given up on the principle of nonviolence. Instead of hoping that blacks and whites would someday "sit down together at the table of brotherhood," as King had mused about in his "I Have a Dream" speech, Carmichael took on an us-versus-them mentality. During the Selma campaign, he had stirred controversy by claiming that blacks should exclude whites from their marches. He would state years later:

> Some negroes have been walking down a dream street talking about sitting next to white people. That does not begin to solve the problem. We didn't go to Mississippi to sit next to [segregationist governor] Ross Barnett, we did not go to sit next to [Selma sheriff] Jim Clark, we went to get them out of our way. People ought to understand that; we were never fighting for the right to integrate, we were fighting against white supremacy.

Carmichael was in Lowndes County (where none of the 12,000 intimidated black citizens were registered to vote in 1964) to help organize the Lowndes County Freedom Organization (LCFO). This all-black political party would be *separate* from the Democratic and Republican parties. Like fellow black nationalists, Carmichael believed that blacks would remain powerless if they comprised a small minority of a nearly all-white political organization. He felt that blacks needed to empower themselves with their own organizations and parties.

While it was legal for African Americans to start their own political party, they were required by law to have a symbol. At the time, the symbol of the Alabama Democratic Party (LCFO) was a white rooster beneath the words "White Supremacy." The LCFO countered the racist rooster with a black panther.

John Hulett, the president of the Lowndes County Christian Movement for Human Rights, became in March 1965 the first black citizen to vote in that county during the twentieth century. He explained why the LCFO chose its symbol:

> The black panther was a vicious animal who, if he was attacked, would not back up. It said that we would fight back if we had to do it. When we chose that symbol, many of the peoples in our county started saying we were a violent group who is going to start killing white folks. But it wasn't that, it was a political symbol that we was here to stay and we were going to do whatever needed to be done to survive.

In Lowndes County, the seeds of the Black Power movement were being planted. LCFO volunteers fanned throughout the county registering African Americans—not as Democrats (as blacks had historically voted) but as members of the new LCFO party. The motto was, "Vote for the panther, then go home."

Many black sharecroppers who did vote for the panther were evicted by white landowners. In March 1966, the LCFO set up a tent city to provide shelter for some of the evicted. By May 1966, some 2,000 black citizens were registered to vote in Lowndes. King's Southern Christian Leadership Conference (SCLC) urged these registered voters to stick with the Democratic Party, but during an election on May 3 some nine hundred blacks in the county voted for LCFO candidates.

All throughout the civil rights movement, the major movement organizations had stuck together: the SCLC, the SNCC, the National Association for the Advancement of Colored People (NAACP), and the Congress for Racial Equality (CORE). But now, with anti-integrationists such as Carmichael gaining prominence, the brotherhood was splintering.

The first major crack took place on May 16, 1966. John Lewis, a devout Christian and a disciple of King, was voted out as the SNCC's

John Lewis, 1964

chairman and replaced by Carmichael. The latter stated at a SNCC meeting that month: "A fundamental change has occurred in the nature of SNCC." He added that the group's new "emphasis must be irrevocably on blackness and black people."

The new SNCC leadership would be much different than that of the civil rights movement leaders, who had followed the peaceful rebellion example of India's Mohandas Gandhi. Stated the *Harvard Crimson* a year later: "The new Howard educated policy-making core—Carmichael, Courtland Cox, Charles Cobb, Cleveland Sellers—focused on the words 'self-determinism,' 'nationalism,' and 'black power.' The newly evolving SNCC image was one of hard cool. The old tactic and credo of Gandhian pacifism was termed irrelevant."

Just three weeks after Carmichael's rise to the top of the SNCC, a gunshot in Mississippi altered the dynamics of the movement. Back in 1962, James Meredith had become the first African American to enroll at the University of Mississippi. Governor Ross Barnett had tried to bar his admission, and rioting in the college town of Oxford was so severe (two dead, 160 injured) that President John F. Kennedy had to call in the National Guard. Meredith graduated from the university, and in June 1966 he staged a "march against fear" from Memphis, Tennessee, to Jackson, Mississippi, to encourage black turnout in Mississippi's June 7 primary election.

During his walk on June 6, Meredith was shot several times by an unemployed white hardware salesman outside of Hernando, Mississippi. While he was hospitalized, King, Carmichael, and Floyd McKissick of CORE flew to Memphis to finish the Meredith **13**

James Meredith, accompanied by U.S. marshals,
walking to class at the University of Mississippi

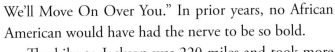

March Against Fear. Eventually, the number of marchers grew to several hundred. One marcher pinned a flier to the back of his shirt that included the LCFO black panther with the words "Move On Over or We'll Move On Over You." In prior years, no African American would have had the nerve to be so bold.

The hike to Jackson was 220 miles and took more than two weeks to complete. On June 17, marchers decided to pitch a sleeping tent on the grounds of a black high school in Greenwood, Mississippi. The police told them not to, but Carmichael tried to erect the tent anyway, leading to his arrest. Word of the story spread throughout the town, and that night nearly 3,000 black citizens attended a rally at a local park.

McKissick, King, and Willie Ricks—who King once referred to as "the fiery orator of SNCC"—spoke to a crowd that was fuming about Carmichael's arrest. SNCC's Cleveland Sellers recalled that "[t]heir speeches were particularly militant." Then, in a dramatic moment, Carmichael arrived after being released from jail. He raised his arm with a clenched fist—a gesture that would become the trademark of the new movement—eliciting a roar from the excited crowd.

The last speaker of the night, Carmichael addressed the mass gathering. "This is the twenty-seventh time I've been arrested—and I ain't going to jail no more!" he cried amid cheers and applause. "The only way we gonna stop them white men from whuppin' us is to take over. We been saying freedom for six years and we ain't got nothin.' What we gonna start saying now is Black Power!"

"Black Power!" the crowd echoed back.

At that moment, Ricks jumped on the platform next to Carmichael and asked the crowd, "What do you want?"

"Black Power!" they cried.

RETALIATION TO CRIME: REVOLUTIONARY VIOLENCE
RÉPONSE AU CRIME: LA VIOLENCE RÉVOLUTIONNAIRE
RESPUESTA AL ASESINATO: VIOLENCIA REVOLUCIONARIA

A 1968 Black Power poster

Again he shouted: "What do you want?"

"Black Power!"

"What do you want?"

"Black Power! Black Power! Black Power!"

From that point on, the Meredith March Against Fear —which would continue until June 26—took on a whole new tone. The day after the Greenwood rally, SNCC members printed mass quantities of Black Power literature. Carmichael continued to call for Black Power, and not even a tear gas attack by police on June 23 in Canton, Mississippi, could subdue the defiant spirit of the activists. Sellers recalled: "At each interview, rally, and press conference, [Carmichael] kept hammering away. . . . Whenever Stokely mounted a platform and asked "What do you want?" they responded without hesitation: "BLACK POWER! BLACK POWER! BLACK POWER!" During such moments, Bob Smith, Willie Ricks and I moved through the crowd distributing Black Power leaflets and placards."

Sellers recalled how Martin Luther King Jr. himself was caught up in the spirit of the march, calling MLK a "staunch ally and a true brother." But during and after the March Against Fear, King and other black leaders pondered the two new words that were on everybody's lips. What exactly did *Black Power* mean? Where would this new mantra and philosophy take the black freedom movement? How would the Ku Klux Klan and other southern whites react to such militant language? And would America as a whole, which had supported the noble and peaceful protests of the civil rights movement, push back against this radical new movement?

All of these important issues would be sorted out in the months and years ahead. But for a people that had been oppressed by whites for more than three hundred years, it felt good just to shout those words from the top of their lungs:

"Black Power!"

Huey P. Newton, national defense minister of the Black Panther Party, raises his clenched fist behind the podium as he speaks at a convention sponsored by the Black Panthers at Temple University in Philadelphia, Pennsylvania, in September 1970. He is surrounded by security guards of the movement.

CHAPTER 2

WHAT EXACTLY WAS BLACK POWER?

In the early 1960s, much of white America admired the black civil rights protesters. "I have always felt that the people of the civil rights movement were the most courageous and inspiring Americans of my generation . . . ," wrote Deborah Rand, a white civil rights activist in the early 1960s. "I was in awe of the sheer beauty of the people who sat down at lunch counters, picketed stores, participated in Freedom Rides, got arrested demanding the right to vote, and demanded that the United States become a real democracy."

By the mid-1960s, however, as some African Americans became more vocally angry about their race's oppression, many white Americans became nervous. Black Americans had revolted in the Watts section of Los Angeles in August 1965, resulting in thirty-four deaths and nine hundred injuries. And in 1966, Stokely Carmichael and other black militants were calling for Black Power.

Whites in major cities with black ghettos—New York, Chicago, Detroit, Cleveland, and others—feared Watts-like uprisings. Some worried that a race war would sweep across the country, with bloody confrontations between white police forces and armed black militants.

What haunted millions of Americans were those two ambiguous words. Reporters persistently asked Carmichael what he had meant by Black Power. "I've given up trying to explain it," he told Gordon Parks in an interview for *Life* magazine. "The whites never really listen when I do anyway." Parks continued to ask for a definition, to which Stokely offered this response:

> *For the last time*, Black Power means black people coming together to form a political force and either electing representatives or forcing representatives to speak their needs. It's an economic and physical bloc that can exercise its strengths in the black community instead of letting the job go to the Democratic or Republican parties or a white-controlled black man set up as a puppet to represent black people. We pick the brother and make sure he fulfills our needs. Black Power doesn't mean anti-white, violence, separatism or any other racist thing the press says it means. It's saying, 'Look, buddy, we're not laying a vote on you unless you lay so many schools, hospitals, playgrounds and jobs on us.'

Despite Stokely's explanations, the public was still confused. There *was* a separatist element to the new movement, and at least the *threat* of violence was often present. As militant SNCC leader H. Rap Brown said in 1967, "If America don't come around, we're gonna burn it down." Moreover, Carmichael's response to Parks's question did not include the new movement's cultural characteristics.

In the 1960s and even today—from a historical perspective—it is difficult to define the Black Power movement. For one thing, it did not have central leadership; instead, many small organizations emerged during the era (1960s and early 1970s), with their own philosophies and agendas. Yet the presence of the Black Power movement was very real, and its impact was enormous.

Hubert Gerald Brown, known as H. Rap Brown,
at a Student Nonviolent Coordinating Committee
news conference in July 1967

21

In short, the Black Power movement arose because many African Americans—who were more educated and enlightened than ever before—fully recognized their oppression and wanted to improve their situation sooner rather than later. Black Power activists believed in self-determination and proactive measures. They strove to create black political parties and black organizations to address issues important to black communities.

One pressing issue involved discrimination in housing and employment. Even though federal law said that companies and individuals couldn't discriminate due to race, white people easily found ways to give jobs to their pals or sell their homes to people who best "fit in" with the neighborhood. Banks tended to view blacks as high-risk candidates for mortgages and loans. African American neighborhoods had poor schools, roads, hospitals, play areas, and so on. Black Power supporters believed that in order to fix these discrepancies, they needed to take bold steps on their own and not wait and hope that the whites in power would make the changes for them.

Self-esteem and pride were critical parts of the new movement. Growing up, black children had been made to feel that they belonged to an inferior race. In Kenneth and Mamie Clark's doll experiments of the 1940s, black children consistently played with white dolls, calling them "good" and "pretty" while referring to the black dolls as "bad" and "ugly." That dreadful self-perception had to change.

Blacks also aimed to establish black studies programs in schools to bolster black pride. African Americans would learn about their heritage and historical achievements—subjects not covered in the regular school curriculum. Many also began wearing African clothing as a means of embracing their African heritage. Similarly, men and women eschewed the hairstyles of white society and let their hair grow naturally. Afros became a highly visible expression of the Black Power movement.

Many Black Power supporters no longer wanted the people of their race to be called *Negroes*. In essence, they felt that the word had too much "baggage"—that it was associated with the days of slavery and segregation. They preferred to call Americans of African descent *black*. "Black is beautiful" became part of the Black Power movement.

The black arts movement, which flourished in the 1960s and 1970s, is considered a branch of the Black Power movement. Blacks established publishing houses, playhouses, dance programs, and art institutions to allow black artists to freely express themselves.

To some extent, white Americans (and many black Americans—particularly the older ones) were unnerved by all of these abrupt changes. But whites were most troubled by two other aspects of the Black Power movement: political ideology and guns.

While white Americans took pride in the principles of democracy and capitalism, many black Americans scoffed at those concepts. Since the country's inception, blacks had been greatly shut out of the country's democratic process. They had been prevented from voting in the Deep South, and few black Americans had ever held significant office. In fact, there were no elected African American governors prior to 1967, and an African American had not been elected to the U.S. Senate since the era of Reconstruction.

As for capitalism, the system rarely worked for black Americans. Some black businesspeople became wealthy, particularly if their establishment was in a northern black community. But most black workers seemingly made half the money of white workers while working twice as hard. Carmichael tells the story of his father:

> The white man says, 'Work hard, nigger, and you'll overcome. . . .' My old man believed in this work-and-overcome stuff. He was religious, never lied, never cheated or stole. He did carpentry all day and drove taxis all night. . . . 'See,' he said, 'have patience and things will come to you.' The next thing that came to that poor black man was death—from working too hard. And he was only in his 40s.

Seeking alternative political and economic situations, most Black Power advocates favored community organizing (taking charge of their neighborhoods) and a national black agenda (which led to the National Black Political Convention in 1972). The more radical Black Power organizations preached elements of communism. Some called for a revolution of the downtrodden against the capitalist oppressors. The Federal Bureau of Investigation (FBI) considered such groups enemies of the state and sought to destroy them, leading to violent, deadly confrontations.

Weapons were another highly controversial aspect of the Black Power movement. Robert F. Williams, a black militant from North Carolina, believed that blacks were justified in buying weapons to defend themselves against the heavily armed Ku Klux Klan. In the late 1960s, Black Panther Party members carried guns in public. They did so, explained party co-founder Huey Newton, after "[w]e had seen the Oakland police and the California Highway Patrol begin to carry their shotguns in full view as another way of striking fear into the community."

The idea of blacks with guns terrified many white Americans and greatly contributed to the downfall of the Black Power movement. Both the FBI and local law enforcement agencies felt that such militant black organizations were a threat to society, and they cracked down hard on them. Repulsed and/or frightened by such militancy—as well as the race riots of the mid- to late 1960s—urban whites fled to the suburbs, leaving cities more impoverished than before. Responding to his law-and-order platform, the American people elected Republican Richard Nixon as president in 1968, ending eight years of liberal leadership.

Mayor Richard Hatcher, the first black mayor of Gary, Indiana, addresses the press at the opening of the National Black Political Convention on March 10, 1972.

A police officer stands at a train depot with
a sign set up to enforce segregation.

CHAPTER 3

THE ROOTS OF BLACK POWER

Though Stokely Carmichael sounded the trumpet for Black Power in Greenwood in 1966, some blacks had been calling for self-determination, separatism, revolution, and the like since the early days of slavery. Malcolm X, a powerful black-rights advocate in the early 1960s, facetiously brought the story back to the Pilgrims, who had landed on Plymouth Rock in 1620. When they arrived, black slaves had been in the colonies for a year. "We didn't land on Plymouth Rock," Malcolm X quipped. "Plymouth Rock landed on us!"

Black Power, in its rawest sense, means blacks working among themselves to improve their destiny. During the era of slavery, such a goal was seemingly impossible—the powers of oppression were too great. Most slaves did not try to escape to freedom in the North because they had no money, no education, and no means of transportation. They also feared retribution, since runaway slaves who were caught were brutally punished.

Nevertheless, early indications of Black Power were seen in mass slave rebellions. In hundreds of documented instances, slaves teamed together—acquiring weapons, orchestrating plans—to escape to freedom and/or seek revenge against their oppressors. With the Underground Railroad, free blacks helped thousands of slaves escape to freedom in the northern states and Canada.

In the mid-1800s, free blacks were among the nation's abolitionists—those who called for the end of slavery. Their persistent agitation—their appeal to the conscience of white northerners through newspaper editorials and public speeches—helped convince President Abraham Lincoln to free the slaves with the Emancipation Proclamation (1863) and helped persuade Congress to pass the Thirteenth, Fourteenth, and Fifteenth Amendments to the Constitution. Those amendments freed the slaves, gave blacks citizenship, and gave black males the right to vote.

Frederick Douglass, a slave who fled to freedom, was an abolitionist and the strongest black voice of the nineteenth century. In April 1865,

Frederick Douglass

with slaves only recently freed, Douglass made a declaration that resonates with the future rhetoric of the Black Power movement. Douglass announced:

Everybody has asked the question . . . 'What shall we do with the Negro?' I have had but one answer from the beginning. Do nothing with us! Your doing with us has already played the mischief with us. . . . If you see him on his way to school, let him alone, don't disturb him! If you see him going to the dinner table at a hotel, let him go! If you see him going to the ballot box, let him alone, don't disturb him! If you see him going into a workshop, just let him alone—your interference is doing him a positive injury.

In the century that followed the Civil War, white America definitely did not leave black people alone—for good or bad. During Reconstruction (1865–1877), the federal government helped rebuild the South while creating opportunities and safeguarding the rights of southern blacks. Most noteworthy, free public schools were made available to black schoolchildren. In addition to the passage of the Thirteenth, Fourteenth, and Fifteenth Amendments, the Civil Rights Act of 1875 prohibited discrimination in public facilities.

Meanwhile, blacks found that they had plenty of white enemies in government. Beginning in 1865, southern legislatures began passing "black codes," which prevented black citizens from renting land, serving on juries, bearing arms, traveling, drinking alcohol, and even learning to read. In 1876, the U.S. Supreme Court ruled that the Fifteenth Amendment did *not* guarantee citizens the right to vote. It listed the grounds impermissible for denying the vote, which indirectly gave southern states ways to *deny* suffrage for black voters.

In 1870, Tennessee mandated the separation of black and white riders on trains. This was the first "Jim Crow" (segregation) law. Throughout the South, seemingly all public facilities became segregated: schools, restaurants, streetcars, outhouses, drinking fountains, swimming pools, theaters, and so on. In virtually every instance, the black facilities were inferior to the white ones. Since only a small percentage of blacks were registered to vote, whites consistently were voted into office—and maintained the laws that oppressed African Americans.

In the Jim Crow South, blacks faced numerous roadblocks to voting: poll taxes that they couldn't afford, constitution tests that were so hard that they couldn't possibly pass them, and threats of job termination. Most African Americans worked menial jobs for pitiful wages. Many were sharecroppers, tending to crops while owing more to the landowner than they were earning.

Under the specter of Jim Crow, the white man called the black man "boy" but insisted on being referred to as "Mister." Blacks could go to jail or be roughed up for the smallest infractions. With such laws as "reckless eyeballing" on the books, a black man dared not even look at a white woman the wrong way. Several thousand black men were lynched by vigilantes in the South, many for interacting with white women. Incredibly, the brazenly unjust system of Jim Crow, begun in the wake of the Civil War, would remain entrenched in the South for close to a hundred years.

Long before the Black Power movement, and even before the modern civil rights movement, black Americans initiated numerous movements in efforts to improve their lives. The Negro Convention movement, dating back to 1830, featured local and national conventions in which free African Americans addressed various black issues. (The 1972 National Black Political Convention, part of the Black Power movement, would be similar in concept.)

In the early 1900s, a philosophical debate raged that was just as heated as the nonviolent/militant debate of the mid-1960s. On one side were the adherents of Booker T. Washington, the founder of Tuskegee Institute (a learning center for young black men and women), and the most prominent African American of his era. Washington urged blacks to let segregation be and to work within the present system. He felt that if blacks learned a skill, worked hard, and bought property, the race would eventually rise above. Whites embraced Washington; in fact, President Theodore Roosevelt even invited him to dinner in 1901. (During the Black Power movement, some activists—fairly or not—would refer to Washington as an "Uncle Tom," a pejorative term meaning one who acts subserviently to whites.)

Intellectual W. E. B. DuBois, the first African American to earn a Ph.D. from Harvard, didn't buy into Washington's philosophy. He criticized Washington's accommodationism—his willingness to let the cycle of white power/black oppression perpetuate itself. In contrast, DuBois believed that black Americans should work to elect black politicians while hammering away at racial discrimination.

In 1905, DuBois and his colleagues initiated the Niagara Movement in Niagara Falls, Canada. He later stated the goals of the movement: "We want full manhood suffrage and we want it now. . . .

A group picture from the first meeting of the Niagara Movement in July 1905

We want discrimination in public accommodation to cease. . . . We want the Constitution of the country enforced."

The Niagara Movement is seen as a precursor to the NAACP, which DuBois helped form in 1909, and the NAACP has direct ties to the modern civil rights movement. Like Martin Luther King Jr.'s movement (and unlike the Black Power movement), the NAACP was open to white members, took pains not to "push too far," and believed in working within the system.

NAACP leaders knew that if they were virulent in their attacks on the white "Establishment"—a term that represented the white domination of corporations, the government, and the military—whites would find ways to shut down the organization. They also didn't push too hard because they relied largely on white philanthropy for their operating expenses. (NAACP leaders would butt heads with DuBois, thinking that he himself was too demanding.)

The Black Power leaders of the 1960s would argue that a black organization could not make significant progress while simultaneously trying to appease white people. The NAACP did have a hard time changing society (their antilynching campaign never resulted in antilynching legislation), but after decades of persistent activism, their efforts began to bear fruit.

Led by attorney Thurgood Marshall, the NAACP won U.S. Supreme Court cases that overturned segregation in graduate schools. In 1954, Marshall won one of the most significant court cases of the twentieth century, *Brown v. Board of Education*, in which the court declared segregated school systems unconstitutional. Chief Justice Earl Warren understood that white schools in the South were always better than the rundown, grossly underfunded black schools. "Separate educational facilities are inherently unequal," Warren asserted.

White southerners referred to the day of the decision as "Black Monday," and many white school systems refused to obey the ruling. Violence against blacks intensified, with the brutal murder of fourteen-year-old Emmett Till in Mississippi in 1955 making headlines nationwide. Over a period of years—well into the 1960s—southern school systems reluctantly but gradually desegregated.

The civil rights movement began in earnest in December 1955, when Rosa Parks was arrested for refusing to yield her seat on a segregated city bus in Montgomery, Alabama. Black citizens responded by boycotting the city's buses. Martin Luther King Jr., who happened to be the pastor of a local Baptist church, was named president of the Montgomery Improvement Association, which oversaw the successful 381-day boycott.

To continue the fight for civil rights, King helped form the Southern Christian Leadership Conference (SCLC). According to their official Web site, the SCLC founders "issued a document declaring that civil rights are essential to democracy, that segregation must end, and that all Black people should reject segregation absolutely and nonviolently."

A segregated bus with white passengers in the
front seats and black passengers in the back

Nonviolence would characterize the civil rights movement. In subsequent bus boycotts in Birmingham, Alabama; Tallahassee, Florida; and elsewhere, boycotters were told to behave like model citizens. If they were caught on camera verbally or physically abusing a white person, local and national public opinion would turn against the black activists and would shatter the goals of the movement.

In 1960 and 1961, thousands of sit-in protesters waited patiently for services at segregated department-store lunch counters and in restaurants throughout the South. The Congress of Racial Equality even staged workshops on proper sit-in etiquette. Even if a white segregationist poured ketchup or soda on a protester, he or she was to remain seated and not respond. The organization that formed out of the sit-in movement included "Nonviolent" as part of its name: the Student Nonviolent Coordinating Committee.

Movement leaders expected similar behavior at all the read-ins (libraries), swim-ins (pools), and other "ins" that were staged in the early to mid-1960s. The SCLC launched mass protest movements in Albany, Georgia; Birmingham; Selma, Alabama; and other cities. By the hundreds, African Americans marched through the streets or waited in line to register to vote. Sometimes they knelt in prayer. Often they were arrested. But virtually never did they strike back. Deliberately playing the role of victim—most noticeably in Birmingham in 1963 (where police unleashed fire hoses and attack dogs on black youths) and then in Selma in 1965—King's movement inspired sympathy and outrage from northern whites and politicians. These tactics led to the Civil Rights Act of 1964 and the Voting Rights Act of 1965.

As the civil rights movement bloomed in the early 1960s, long-standing fears of southern whites were realized. Throughout slavery and beyond, many whites had wanted to minimize the education of blacks as much as possible. The more blacks read, the whites reasoned, the more they would be aware of the gross injustice inflicted upon them. This is why Frederick Douglass's normally mild-mannered master flew off the handle when he found that his wife was teaching Frederick to read. It is why southern textbooks dared not mention the sins of southern history. Black education was so under-funded, and learning so discouraged, that in 1960 only 20 percent of African Americans had a high school diploma and only 3 percent had graduated from college.

In the 1960s, however, black Americans became far more informed, particularly about social issues. The reasons for this "black enlight-enment" were numerous. At the time, stories about the civil rights movement dominated the media, especially black-owned newspapers and magazines such as the *Chicago Defender* and *Jet*. Preachers railed against white oppression from their pulpits, and race was the center-piece of discussions in barbershops and at the kitchen table.

Every time African Americans heard about white retaliation—such as the bombing of King's home during the Montgomery bus boycott or the 1963 church bombing in Birmingham that killed four girls—they became angrier and more determined to fight for their rights.

Lew Alcindor, who would go on to become the NBA's career scor-ing leader as Kareem Abdul-Jabbar, remembered how moved he was by the Emmett Till story: "The murder shocked me," he wrote. "I began thinking of myself as a black person for the first time, not just a per-son. And I grew more distrustful and wary. I remember thinking: They killed him because of his color. In a way, I lost my childish innocence."

As the sit-ins spread like wildfire in 1960, they ignited a fire within the black youth of America. Stokely Carmichael recalled: "When I first heard about the Negroes sitting in at lunch counters down South, I thought they were just a bunch of publicity hounds. But one night when I saw those young kids on TV, getting back up on the lunch counter stools after being knocked off them, sugar in their eyes, ketch-up in their hair—well, something happened to me. Suddenly I was burning."

Outraged by the injustice they witnessed, young blacks joined the civil rights movement by the thousands. They attended meetings and rallies, where the rhetoric became stronger in tone. "I've got vengeance in my heart tonight," CORE's David Dennis said at the funeral of **35** black activist James Chaney in Mississippi in 1964. "Those neighbors who were too afraid to come to this service, pick them up and take them down there to register to vote! . . . Just tell them: 'Baby, I'm here! Stand up! Hold your heads up! Don't bow down anymore! We want our freedom now!'"

In the 1960s, more blacks attended college, where they were more inclined to read about social injustice. For the first time, many began to read books by black leaders with alternative views.

They read about Marcus Garvey, an early twentieth-century figure who had very different views than King, the NAACP, and the other mainstream civil rights organizations had. A union organizer from Jamaica, Garvey moved to Harlem in 1916. He was a black nationalist, believing that blacks would never be accepted into white society and, therefore, should remove themselves from that society. As the founder and leader of the Universal Negro Improvement Association, Garvey formed the Black Star Line, a steamship company dedicated to sending African Americans to Africa. Financial problems ruined his plans, but Garvey remained an icon to succeeding generations of black nationalists.

In 1954, esteemed African American author Richard Wright published *Black Power*. The nonfiction book chronicled the developments in Africa's Gold Coast, where its people—with the cry of "self-government now"—demanded freedom from British colonialism. Ghana would declare independence in 1957, and in 1960 seventeen other African nations would achieve independence. These victories in Africa had a significant effect on the leaders of the civil rights and Black Power movements. Martin Luther King Jr. went to Ghana in 1957, and Malcolm X met with three presidents of freedom-fighting nations. Medgar Evers, an NAACP field secretary in Mississippi, said in 1963 (just three weeks before a segregationist assassinated him), "Tonight the Negro knows . . . that a Congo native can be a locomotive engineer, but in Jackson, he cannot even drive a garbage truck."

The civil rights movement opposed the use of violence even when black people felt threatened. Robert F. Williams, president of the

The Rev. Martin Luther King Jr. (left) and Malcom X meet before a press conference. Both men had come to hear the Senate debate on the Civil Rights Act of 1964.

NAACP chapter in Monroe, North Carolina, didn't buy in to this line of reasoning. With the Ku Klux Klan staking a strong presence in Monroe, Williams pronounced his intention to meet violence with violence. Those in his chapter armed themselves with machine guns and dynamite. Williams's book *Negroes with Guns* (1962) would have a profound influence on Huey P. Newton, co-founder of the most famous Black Power organization, the Black Panther Party, which would advocate the use of guns in self-defense.

The Nation of Islam (NOI), formed in 1930, captured the nation's attention in the 1960s—especially when outspoken boxing champion Cassius Clay joined their ranks and changed his name (in 1964) to Muhammad Ali. The NOI believed in the Holy Qur'an as well as the Bible, although they believed that the latter "has been tampered with and must be reinterpreted." This black separatist organization would have a strong impact on the Black Power movement. And, the organization's beliefs that relate to race were at the core of its mission:

7. WE BELIEVE this is the time in history for the separation of the so-called Negroes and the so-called white Americans. We believe the black man should be freed in name as well as in fact. By this we mean that he should be freed from the names imposed upon him by his former slave masters. Names that identified him as being the slave master's slave. We believe that if we are free indeed, we should go in our own people's names—the black people of the Earth.

8. WE BELIEVE in justice for all, whether in God or not; we believe as others, that we are due equal justice as human beings. We believe in equality—as a nation—of equals. We do not believe that we are equal with our slave masters in the status of freed slaves.

We recognize and respect American citizens as independent peoples and we respect their laws which govern this nation.

9. WE BELIEVE that the offer of integration is hypocritical and is made by those who are trying to deceive the black peoples into believing that their 400-year-old open enemies of freedom, justice, and equality are, all of a sudden, their "friends." Furthermore, we believe that such deception is intended to prevent black people from realizing that the time in history has arrived for the separation from the whites of this nation.

Malcolm X was the most outspoken member of the Nation of Islam. Born Malcolm Little in 1925, he grieved as a child over his father's death. He believed that a white supremacist group had killed Earl Little because of his work on behalf of Marcus Garvey.

Malcolm's criminal behavior landed him in prison, where he joined the Nation of Islam. As a young NOI minister, stated *Civil Rights Chronicle*, he "quickly earned a reputation for his forceful, cogent calls for black pride and militancy."

Tall and bespectacled, with a strong jaw and a piercing gaze, Malcolm X stood up for African Americans without hedging his words to appease whites. "Nobody can give you freedom," he declared. "Nobody can give you equality or justice or anything. If you're a man, you take it."

Malcolm had mixed feelings about the civil rights movement. He applauded the efforts of the activists who marched and sat in for justice, but he didn't like the notion of blacks sacrificing themselves just for the hope that whites in Washington would bestow new laws upon them. He referred to the 1963 March on Washington as nothing more than a "picnic," and he had plenty to say on the issue of nonviolence. "Nonviolence is fine as long as it works," he stated. He denounced Martin Luther King Jr.'s turn-the-other-cheek philosophy when he declared: "Be peaceful, be courteous, obey the law, respect everyone; but if someone puts his hand on you, send him to the cemetery."

By 1964, he rivaled King as the most influential voice in black America. Malcolm left the Nation of Islam that year after a feud with NOI leaders, and afterward his militant, separatist views began to soften. In early 1965, he attempted to bridge the ideological gap between him and King when he spoke at Brown Chapel in Selma, Alabama.

On February 21, Malcolm X was assassinated by NOI members. However, his influence on black America remained strong even in death. *The Autobiography of Malcolm X*, published later in 1965, would be hailed as one of the most influential books of the twentieth century. In the mid- and late 1960s, many black Americans would take Malcolm's mantra—"by any means necessary"—to heart.

Author James Baldwin also had an impact on the Black Power movement. The son of a Harlem storefront preacher, Baldwin frequently wrote about social injustice and prejudice. In his book *The Fire Next Time*, he predicted the violent turn that the civil rights movement would take. "The Negroes of this country may never be able to rise to power," he wrote, "but they are very well placed indeed to precipitate chaos and ring down the curtain on the American dream."

The changing attitudes of black society were reflected in the 1965 heavyweight championship bout between the aging Floyd Patterson and the young champion, Muhammad Ali. Patterson was a mild-mannered African American with a squeaky-clean image. The famously opinionated Ali called Patterson an Uncle Tom. He had this to say about himself: "I am America. I am the part you won't recognize. But get used to me. Black, confident, cocky. My name, not yours. My religion, not yours. My goals, my own. Get used to me."

Ali, by the way, won the fight.

Meanwhile, black anger was beginning to boil over in urban areas. Wrote civil rights historian Todd Burroughs, "The conditions for insurrections in black communities were already present in too many American cities: bad housing, bad schools, police brutality, and lack of economic opportunity. In Chicago in 1965, for instance, African-Americans held only five percent of the city's 'professional' jobs."

In Harlem on July 16, 1964, a white police lieutenant fatally shot a fifteen-year-old boy, triggering a race riot (or insurrection, depending on one's perspective). That same year, riots raged in Philadelphia; Paterson and Jersey City, New Jersey; and Dixmoor, Illinois. In Philadelphia, approximately one hundred police officers were injured.

When a fire truck fatally hit a black woman in Chicago on August 12, 1965, it might have been an accident. But tensions were so high that two nights of rioting erupted. A day earlier, a much worse scenario exploded in the Watts section of Los Angeles, where a heat wave had everyone on edge. A rumor of police brutality was the spark that caused "the fire" that Baldwin had predicted.

For six days, an estimated 35,000 African Americans rioted in Watts. Entire blocks were burned to the ground, and blacks fired guns at police, fire fighters, and even airplanes. One person planted a home-made sign in the middle of the street that stated, chillingly, "Turn Left or Get Shot." Law enforcement officials and the National Guard eventually achieved peace, but the casualties included thirty-four dead and some nine hundred injured.

Though he had long focused his attention on southern racism, Martin Luther King Jr. flew to Los Angeles, where he called for a civil review board to address police brutality—which L.A. police chief William H. Parker resented.

In the summer of 1966, King and the SCLC launched the Chicago Freedom Movement in Chicago as a first step in addressing the problems of the northern ghettos. They made little progress. During a march, a white counter-protester threw a rock that struck King in the head. "I have never in my life seen such hate," King said. Chicago mayor Richard Daley closed City Hall when he heard that blacks were marching there. King responded by taping a list of demands on a City Hall door.

It was becoming clear that King's influence had peaked with the Selma campaign, and that black activists wanted more, faster, than what King's gradualist movement was used to delivering. King's earlier declaration to whites—"we will wear you down by our capacity to suffer"—was outdated. Instead, a growing number of young blacks embraced the philosophy of Stokely Carmichael, who elicited cries of "Black Power!" at the 1966 rallies in Mississippi.

Despite dissension within their ranks, the SNCC—with Carmichael as their leader—was on board with Black Power. So too was CORE, one of the major civil rights groups. The militant Floyd

A photograph taken on August 15, 1965, of one of many buildings looted and burned during the riot in Watts

McKissick became CORE's leader in 1966, and that summer he hoisted a "Black Power" sign during a protest in New York City.

Meanwhile, the other major civil rights groups condemned the new direction in which the young radicals were taking the movement. The NAACP, perhaps the most conservative of the civil rights groups, wanted nothing to do with Black Power. Bayard Rustin, the chief organizer of the March on Washington, wrote: "'Black power' not only lacks any real value for the civil rights movement, but its propagation is positively harmful. It diverts the movement from a meaningful debate over strategy and tactics, it isolates the Negro community, and it encourages the growth of anti-Negro forces."

A. Philip Randolph, who had threatened a march on Washington in 1941 and helped lead the 1963 march, denounced Black Power. He called it a philosophy "based upon the assumption of salvation through racial isolation." He warned the new militants to "take great care against overheating the ghettos"; otherwise, they could erupt into "a race war in this nation which could become catastrophic."

King had plenty to say on the topic. He did not think that "Black Power" was a smart choice of words, saying they could cause confusion and alarm. Like Rustin and Randolph, he feared a white backlash. King stated: "Anyone leading a violent rebellion must be willing to make an honest assessment regarding the possible casualties to a minority population confronting a well-armed wealthy majority with a fanatical right wing that would delight in exterminating thousands of black men, women, and children."

Despite sounding this alarm, King, in his 1967 book *Where Do We Go From Here: Chaos or Community?*, also acknowledged that the new movement was inevitable: "I guess I should not have been surprised. I should have known that in an atmosphere where false promises are daily realities, where deferred dreams are nightly facts, where acts of unpunished violence toward Negroes are a way of life, nonviolence would eventually be seriously questioned."

Entering 1967, white America hoped that the uprisings in Watts and other cities had been isolated incidents—that the cries of "Black Power" in Mississippi had just been voices in the wind. However, when thirty militant-looking black men and women, carrying exposed firearms, marched on the California statehouse in May 1967, white Americans sat up in attention. Black Power was more than just rhetoric.

A National Guardsman stands at the ready at a Detroit intersection during the summer riots of 1967. Detroit was one of several northern cities where black frustration and despair erupted into rage and violence.

CHAPTER 4

BLACK MILITANCY

On May 2, 1967, a six-car caravan of Black Panthers pulled up to the California Capitol building. Thirty of them, led by Black Panther Party chairman Bobby Seale, got out of the cars. Twenty of them carried guns, including long-barreled shotguns. With wide-eyed whites gawking at them from a distance, the Panthers loaded their weapons.

"All right, brothers," Seale said, "let's roll."

As they walked toward the Capitol, the Panthers made sure to point their guns either up or down. By doing so they would stay within the parameters of California law, which they did not want to violate. Seale and his group were not there to hurt anyone. Instead, they wanted to make a high-profile protest of the pending Mulford Act, which the California Assembly was scheduled to discuss on that day. The Mulford Act would prohibit the carrying of firearms in public places in California.

Seale's goals were to reach the visitor area of the Assembly and—in front of reporters and film crews—read the Black Panthers' "Executive Mandate Number 1," which explained why the Mulford Act was a racist law.

Never in American history had there been a scene like this. Out in the distance, Governor Ronald Reagan was speaking on the Capitol lawn to two hundred Future Youth, Future Leaders (ironically, an all- or predominantly white group). When Reagan's entourage saw the armed militants in the distance, they told the governor to immediately leave.

"Look at Reagan run," one of the Panthers said.

Seale led the Panthers into the Capitol, where reporters ran up to them and everyone else got out of their way. "Man they were shocked," Seale wrote. "They moved and stepped aside, and I saw some of their mouths hanging open, just looking, and they were saying with their eyes and their faces and their expressions, 'Who in the hell are these niggers with these guns?'"

Seale and the Panthers eventually reached the Assembly, which was indeed in session. Amid the uproar that developed, Seale focused his contempt on the police—who black militants were now referring to as "pigs"—and the few black assemblymen. "I looked at those bootlickers, those Uncle Toms, very intensely," Seale wrote. "I didn't care for them because they never represented us there."

After confrontations with police, the Panthers left the building— but not before Seale read the mandate. His opening statement summed up why they were there that day:

> The Black Panther Party for Self-Defense calls upon the American people in general and the Black people in particular to take careful note of the racist California Legislature, which is now considering legislation aimed at keeping the Black people disarmed and powerless at the very same time that racist police agencies throughout the country are intensifying the terror, brutality, murder and repression of Black people.

An eagle, the national emblem of the United States of America and a symbol of freedom, adorns the Capitol Building in Sacramento, California

The mandate stated that police dogs, cattle prods, and increased patrols had become familiar sights in black communities. The mandate also offered a perspective on American history that certainly wasn't presented in the history textbooks of the day:

> The enslavement of black people at the very founding of this country, the genocide practiced on the American Indians and the confining of the survivors on reservations, the savage lynching of thousands of black men and women, the dropping of atomic bombs on Hiroshima and Nagasaki, and now the cowardly massacre in Vietnam, all testify to the fact that toward people of color the racist power structure of America has but one policy: repression, genocide, terror, and the big stick.

After May 2, the whole country was aware of the Black Panther Party (BPP), which Seale and Huey Newton had co-founded in October 1966. In some ways, the Black Panther Party was an outgrowth of the SNCC. They shared the same Black Power mantra that SNCC leader Stokely Carmichael preached, and they borrowed the Black Panther symbol from the SNCC's voter registration project in Lowndes County, Alabama. The Panthers, however, focused their attention on urban areas.

Upon the Black Panther Party's founding, Seale and Newton listed ten demands in their "Platform and Program of the Black Panther Party." They included, verbatim:

1. We want freedom. We want power to determine the destiny of our Black Community.

2. We want full employment for our people.

3. We want an end to the robbery by the white man of our Black Community.

4. We want decent housing, fit for shelter of human beings.

5. We want education for our people that exposes the true nature of this decadent American society. We want education that teaches us our true history and our role in the present-day society.

6. We want all black men to be exempt from military service.

7. We want an immediate end to police brutality and murder of black people.

8. We want freedom for all black men held in federal, state, county and city prisons and jails.

9. We want all black people when brought to trial to be tried in court by a jury of their peer group or people from their black communities, as defined by the Constitution of the United States.

10. We want land, bread, housing, education, clothing, justice and peace. And as our major political objective, a United Nations-supervised plebiscite to be held throughout the black colony in which only black colonial subjects will be allowed to participate for the purpose of determining the will of black people as to their national destiny.

For each demand, Seale and Newton wrote an explanation. For example, they believed that blacks should be exempt from the military (Point 6) because "[w]e will not fight and kill other people of color in the world who, like black people, are being victimized by the white racist government of America." They believed that all black men should be released from jails and prisons (Point 8) "because they have not received a fair and impartial trial."

Much of the Panthers' rhetoric was Marxist in tone. Karl Marx, a nineteenth-century German philosopher and social scientist, believed that in a capitalist society, an economic minority (bourgeoisie) dominated and exploited the majority (proletariat). Marx believed that an international social revolution of the masses was needed to overcome the injustice. To achieve equality for all, he believed, the productive capacities of society should be placed in collective ownership.

Points 2 and 4 of the Panthers' platform (employment and housing) were clearly Marxist in nature. In Point 4, the platform stated: "We believe that if the white landlords will not give decent housing to our black community, then the housing and the land should be made into cooperatives so that our community, with government aid, can build and make decent housing for its people."

Marxism was the basis of communism, and since World War II the United States had waged a Cold War with the Soviet Union to stop the spread of communism. America's main goal for both the Korean War and the Vietnam War was to contain communism, and for decades the FBI relentlessly tried to eliminate any domestic organization that resembled communism. Because of the Panthers' communist leanings, not to mention their militant, anti-Establishment stance, the FBI was determined to decimate them. Eventually, the FBI would succeed in its mission, but not before the Black Panther Party would grow in popularity.

In black communities, Seale, Newton, and fellow Panther Eldridge Cleaver became household names. The son of a carpenter, Seale did not make his high school football and basketball teams, he said, because of racial prejudice. After three years in the Air Force, he was court-martialed for disobeying a colonel. While in college, he was drawn to the words of Malcolm X as well as the Afro-American Association, which emphasized black separatism and self-improvement. Feeling that the organization did not do enough to battle political and economic oppression, Seale and Huey Newton formed the Black Panther Party for Self-Defense in October 1966.

The son of a Baptist minister, Newton graduated from Oakland Technical High School not knowing how to read. Once he taught himself to read, he absorbed the writings of far-left leaders Karl Marx, Malcolm X, and Mao Zedong (the chairman of communist China). From adolescence through college, Newton indulged in crime, including multiple burglaries.

Such a biography would draw the ire of most patriotic Americans. Yet in his book *Revolutionary Suicide*, Newton garners empathy with his honesty and insights:

> As I suffered through Sambo and the Black Tar Baby story in *Brer Rabbit* in the early grades, a great weight began to settle on me. It was the weight of ignorance and inferiority imposed by the system. I found myself wanting to identify with the white heroes in the primers and in the movies I saw, and in time I cringed at the mention of Black. This created a gulf of hostility between the teachers and me, a lot of it repressed, but still there, like the strange mixture of hate and admiration we Blacks felt toward whites generally.

> We simply did not feel capable of learning what the white kids could learn. . . . Our image of ourselves was defined for us by textbooks and teachers. We not only accepted ourselves as inferior; we accepted the inferiority as inevitable and inescapable.

. . . Predictably, this sense of despair and futility led us into rebellious attitudes. Rebellion was the only way we knew to cope with the suffocating, repressive atmosphere that undermined our confidence.

Later in the book, Newton explains why he and Seale formed the Black Panther Party. They did so, he states, in reaction to the Oakland police and California Highway Patrol, which had begun "to carry their shotguns in full view as another way of striking fear into the community. We had seen all this, and we recognized that the rising consciousness of Black people was almost at the point of explosion. Out of this sprang the Black Panther Party."

Huey Newton

The "explosion" that Newton anticipated became a reality in the spring and summer of 1967. On May 11, just nine days after the Panthers' march on the California Capitol, protesters stormed a police barricade at Jackson State College in Mississippi. Authorities responded with gunfire, killing one. A student's arrest at all-black Texas Southern University on May 16 led to campus unrest, resulting in the arrest of five hundred students.

But the deadliest insurrection of the decade raged in Detroit from June 23 to 28, triggering what came to be known as America's "long, hot summer." In Detroit, unbearably hot weather, the killing of an African American Army veteran by police, and raids on black after-hours social clubs (called "blind pigs") had the black community on edge.

When an officer smashed the window of a social club with a sledgehammer, the uprising began. By the time the National Guard had restored order, forty-three people (thirty-three black) lay dead, 1,300 buildings had been burned, and 7,200 people (6,400 black) had been arrested.

During and after the riot, blacks and whites offered completely different perspectives. Blacks explained why the riot happened, while whites focused on the violence of the rioters. Said Ron Scott, who would cofound the Detroit Black Panther Party:

> Inside of most black people there was a time bomb. There was a pot that was about to overflow, and there was rage that was about to come out. And the rebellion just provided an opportunity for that. I mean, why else would people get upset, cops raiding a blind pig. They'd done that numerous times before. But people just got tired, people just got tired of it. And it just exploded.

Eleanor Josaitis was a white civil rights worker living in the predominantly white, working-class suburb of Taylor. She and her neighbors watched the rioting on TV. She recalled, "Television showed pictures of people in the street, it showed burning, it showed buildings on fire, it showed total confusion, it showed tanks coming into the city, it showed troops, it showed people looting. It looked like a war-torn zone. . . . And again, the negative comments about [black] people, and the name-callings—'animal' was the favorite term."

With tensions boiling in the summer of 1967, just one incident could spark a citywide riot. That's what happened on July 12 in the working-class city of Newark, New Jersey. The police beating of black

Hundreds of people charge down Twelfth Street on Detroit's West Side on July 23, 1967, throwing stones and bottles at storefronts and looting them.

cab driver John Smith triggered a five-day insurrection in which twenty-six people were killed. Blacks in Newark vented their anger over chronic racial profiling and police brutality, the lack of black political representation in a city that was mostly African American, and the uprooting of a black neighborhood for the construction of a state teaching hospital center.

In the minds of many black Newarkers, whites were trying to oppress the city's black population. Wrote white left-wing activist Tom Hayden: "The city's vast programs for urban renewal, highways, downtown development, and most recently, a 150 acre Medical School in the heart of the ghetto seemed almost deliberately designed to squeeze out this rapidly growing Negro community that represents a majority of the population."

All told during the "long, hot summer," scores of riots erupted across the country, resulting in some one hundred deaths. From New York City and Buffalo to Milwaukee and Minneapolis to Birmingham and Tampa, black residents "took it to the streets."

An aerial view of fire fighters trying to extinguish fires caused by the riots in Newark, New Jersey, on July 14, 1967

Then and now, sociologists have debated whether the Black Power movement "caused" the rioting. Supporters of the movement deny the accusation, claiming that generations of discrimination and oppression were the root causes. They believe that the movement merely enlightened African Americans and encouraged them to stand up, proudly, for their rights.

Others believe that the movement did spark the riots. They note that many in the movement took up arms (albeit in self-defense, according to the Panthers) and called for revolution. They point to the rhetoric of H. Rap Brown, the new radical leader of the SNCC. On July 24, 1967, he proclaimed in a speech in Cambridge, Maryland: "I see all them stores sitting up there and all them honkies owns them. You got to own some of them stores. I don't care if you have to burn him down and run him out. You'd better take over them stores."

Shortly afterward, black arsonists rampaged in a local black district, leaving two blocks of buildings in ruins. In this case, the connection between Black Power rhetoric and black insurrection was so strong that

Brown was arrested for inciting the rioting. Maryland governor Spiro Agnew announced, "It shall now be the policy of this state to immediately arrest any person inciting to riot, and to not allow that person to finish his vicious speech."

It is noteworthy, however, that a federal commission blamed whites, not blacks, for the summer of rioting. On July 28, 1967, President Lyndon Johnson initiated the National Advisory Commission on Civil Disorders to study the root causes of the summer's insurrections. Headed by Illinois governor Otto Kerner, the commission released its findings—known as the "Kerner Report"—a year later.

The report boldly and famously stated: "This is our basic conclusion. Our nation is moving toward two societies, one black, one white—separate and unequal." The report also stated, "Discrimination and segregation have long permeated much of American life; they now threaten the future of every American."

As for the causes of the riots, the commission pointed to the following: deeply embedded racism, great frustration by inner-city African Americans, police brutality and profiling, high unemployment, chronic poverty, poor housing and schools, and lack of access to health care.

Those who claimed that the commission was biased in its assessment didn't have much ground to stand on. Of the eleven commission members, only two were black (NAACP executive director Roy Wilkins and U.S. senator Edward Brooke). Of the commission's six politicians, three were Democrats and three were Republicans. The group also included the police chief of Atlanta and the president of the United Steelworkers of America.

The Kerner Report recommended that the federal government try to remedy the inner-city ills. It suggested improvements in education, employment, housing, and public services, and it even called for a national system of income supplementation. Ironically, the recommendations of this mostly white federal commission resonated with the Black Panthers' Ten-Point Program. Although the Fair Housing Act, passed in April 1968, prohibited discrimination in housing, President Johnson would not directly act on the commission's findings.

Meanwhile, African Americans sought to take control of their future. A week after the Newark riot, black nationalists and black mainstream reformists convened for the second Newark Black Power Conference. According to civil rights historian Todd Burroughs, "The most significant accomplishment was Newark activist/poet Amiri Baraka's establishment of the United Brothers, a group that would evolve into the Committee for Unified Newark." The new organization would run black candidates for public office, an effort that would result in the mayoral election of African American Kenneth Gibson in 1970. This was what Black Power was all about: black citizens working together to empower their communities.

In 1968, black nationalist Floyd McKissick left CORE to launch a new community, Soul City, on farmland in Warren County, North Carolina. McKissick envisioned a self-contained, integrated community that included an industrial center, schools, health care facilities, and places of worship. The federal government would grant $14 million to the Soul City project in 1972, but it would ultimately be a failed enterprise.

In riot-torn Detroit, black autoworkers empowered themselves through unionization. At Chrysler's Hamtramck assembly plant, black workers formed the Dodge Revolutionary Union Movement (DRUM). In the DRUM newsletter, they explained that 60 percent of the union workers were black but more than 90 percent of the plant's foremen, superintendents, and skilled tradesmen were white. "Systematically all the easy jobs in the plants are held by whites," the newsletter stated, and "[w]henever whites are put on harder jobs they are given helpers."

For three days in July 1968, DRUM staged a 4,000-worker strike at the plant, preventing the production of some 3,000 cars. The black union's defiance caused a ruckus among white workers, the UAW, and Chrysler executives, but DRUM stood strong. In the next union election, they ran their own slate of black candidates.

Taking their cues from DRUM, black workers at the Ford River Rouge Plant formed FRUM (Ford Revolutionary Union Movement), and those at the Chrysler Eldon Avenue plant established ELRUM (Eldon Avenue Revolutionary Union Movement). Similar "RUMs" were formed at the United Parcel Service and among health workers. In 1969, these organizations would merge to form the League of Revolutionary Black Workers (LRBW), which lasted for two years before splintering into other groups.

Few in mainstream America were aware of these black unions, but seemingly everybody knew about the group with the big guns, the Black Panthers. The organization was often in the media, especially after an incident on October 28, 1967.

While driving in Oakland before dawn, Panthers co-founder Huey Newton was pulled over by police officer John Frey. According to Newton's testimony, Frey greeted him by saying, "Well, well, well, what do we have? The great, great Huey P. Newton." After Newton was asked to get out of the car, an argument, a scuffle, and shootings followed. Amid the chaos, Newton, Frey, and backup officer Herbert Heanes were all shot, with Frey dying from his wounds. Newton, with a bullet wound to the abdomen, made it to Kaiser Hospital, where he was chained to a bed.

Despite sketchy evidence, Newton was arrested and, in July 1968, went on trial for the killing of Frey. That September, Newton's loyal followers were appalled when he was convicted of voluntary manslaughter. Black Panther chapters staged rallies around the country. Donning Afros and raising clenched fists, supporters chanted, "Free Huey! Off the pigs!" "Off the pigs" meant "kill the police," causing alarm and disgust among conservative Americans.

Nevertheless, the Panthers became remarkably popular among young African Americans. Its newspaper, the *Black Panther*, reached a peak circulation of 400,000. Many young blacks were moved by the writings of Eldridge Cleaver, the Panthers' minister of information.

Born in 1935, Cleaver spent 1957 to 1966 behind bars for the rapes of multiple women, black and white. While incarcerated at Folsom

Kathleen Cleaver (center), wife of Eldridge Cleaver, and Bobby Seale at the "Free Huey" demonstration in Oakland, California, in 1969

Prison in California, he wrote a series of essays that would comprise his 1968 best-selling book *Soul on Ice*. The essays touched on many racial themes, including the perception of black and white men in America. According to Cleaver, black men played the roles of "Supermasculine Menials" while white men were "Omnipotent Administrators." The analogy (which resonates with the slave-master relationship) made sense to *Soul on Ice* readers, for in the 1960s white men still dominated corporate boardrooms and political offices.

Cleaver's blunt honesty and unique perspectives earned raves from left-wing critics and condemnation from conservatives—particularly because of his explanation of why he had raped white women: "It delighted me that I was defying and trampling upon the white man's law, upon his system of values, and that I was defiling his women." When the University of California at Berkeley asked Cleaver to speak there, conservative California governor Ronald Reagan said, "If Eldridge Cleaver is allowed to teach our children, they may come home one night and slit our throats."

Such conflicts and anxieties characterized America in the 1960s. The United States had been largely a patriotic, conservative nation until the eruption of the civil rights movement and the rebellion against the Vietnam War. While black militants already despised the white "establishment," the war caused young whites to hate the Establishment as well. Why, they felt, should they be drafted at age eighteen and shipped to faraway jungles to kill and be killed? On college campuses and elsewhere, angry students (mostly white but blacks as well) burned draft cards and staged massive antiwar rallies.

Black militants were especially incensed that black soldiers were dying at a disproportionately higher rate than whites on the Vietnam battlefields. They felt that black Americans shouldn't be there at all. Stokely Carmichael handed out bitterly satirical leaflets that said: "Support White Power—travel to Viet Nam, you might get a medal!"; "Die Nigger Die—you can't die fast enough in the ghettos"; and "Receive valuable training in the skills of killing off other oppressed people!"

Martin Luther King Jr. also strongly decried the war. Like Carmichael, he wondered why black men were being sent to the front lines "to guarantee liberties in Southeast Asia which they had not found in southwest Georgia and East Harlem."

Many black soldiers, especially Black Power supporters, deeply resented being drafted. Soldier Robert McCarthy of Newark told a *United Press International* reporter exactly how he felt. "The black man ain't gonna fight for the rabbit [white man]," he said. "We don't got nothing against Charlie [the Vietnamese]. Man, he ain't white either. If the white man wants to kill Charlie, he can do it himself."

With Newton incarcerated, Bobby Seale helped turn the Black Panthers from a local organization into a national one. He also played a leading role in the massive antiwar protest at the 1968 Democratic National Convention in Chicago, which culminated in a bloody street battle between protesters and club-wielding police officers. Seale was one of the "Chicago Eight" who were subsequently tried for inciting rioting at the convention.

During his trial, Seale shouted accusations and insults at Judge Julius Hoffman, at one point calling him a "blatant racist." Marshals responded to Seale's courtroom outbursts by tying rags around his mouth and shackling him to his chair with handcuffs and leg irons. In a startling show of defiance, Seale continued to protest by banging his handcuffs against his chair and voicing a muffled "I object" over and over.

Seale was immortalized in the 1971 Graham Nash song "Chicago," an antiwar anthem that opens with these lyrics: "Though your brother's bound and gagged / And they've chained him to a chair . . . In a land that's known as freedom/How can such a thing be fair."

At the 1968 Summer Olympics in Mexico City, the Black Power movement went international. After finishing first and third respectively in the 200-meter sprint, Tommie Smith and John Carlos arrived at the victory stand in bare feet—to represent the slavery and discrimination that black Americans had endured—and wearing civil rights buttons. They also wore black, skin-tight gloves, which they used to give the Black Power salute. The International Olympic Committee was aghast, and the U.S. Organizing Committee ordered the two men to leave the Olympic Village, stating that political expression was not allowed in the Games.

Team USA's gold and bronze medalists Tommie Smith (center) and John Carlos (right) raise their arms as a Black Power gesture during the 1968 Olympic awards ceremony in Mexico City.

Smith later explained why he gave the salute. "People thought the victory stand was a hate message," he said. "But it wasn't. It was a cry for freedom."

Also in 1968, two Detroit-based black militant organizations attempted to sever ties with white America once and for all. The Malcolm X Society and the Group on Advanced Leadership (GOAL) proposed the creation of the Republic of New Afrika. In a weekend meeting that spring, five hundred black nationalists created a Declaration of Independence and a constitution for their republic. They sought to control the land of five states (Mississippi, Alabama, Georgia, Louisiana, and South Carolina) and other black-majority counties in the South and elsewhere. As compensation for slavery and economic discrimination over the centuries, the republic sought billions of dollars in reparations from the U.S. government.

The Republic of New Afrika was short-lived, but other black militants promulgated the concept of reparations—and not just from the government. On May 11, 1969, former SNCC organizer James Forman, on behalf of the National Black Economic Development Conference (NBEDC), read his "Black Manifesto" outside Riverside Church in New York City. Forman demanded that white Christian churches and Jewish synagogues pay $500 million for taking part in perpetrating slavery. "Time is running out," Forman said. "We have been slaves too long. The Church is racist. The Church has profited from our labor. We are men and women, proud black men and women. Our demands shall be met."

In *Reparations for Slavery: A Reader*, authors Ronald P. Salzberger and Mary Turck speculated that NBEDC leaders thought they would have better luck convincing churches to pay reparations than the government. The manifesto indicated how the $500 million would be spent. It would go to the establishment of a black university; cooperative farms to help poor, rural blacks; black-themed publishing companies; black television networks; and "a research skills center which will provide research on the problems of black people." Forman's dreams were never realized, however, as religious groups almost universally denounced the Black Manifesto.

Black Power advocates had more luck when it came to black studies—although they often had to press the issue. In the late 1960s, the black studies movement swept college campuses nationwide. African American students demanded the establishment of classes that emphasized the history and social concerns of black Americans—instead of relying on the traditional curriculums, which largely ignored such subject matter.

Universities often balked at or reacted slowly to the militants' demands. According to school officials, establishing a black studies program took time, cost too much money, or wasn't fully necessary. Black studies activists would not tolerate such stonewalling, resulting in numerous confrontations.

On February 27, 1969, 3,000 students at the University of Wisconsin in Madison gathered to demand a black studies program. On April 22, 1969, black and Puerto Rican students at the City College of New York chained the gates of the south campus, causing the school to shut down for days.

That same month, some one hundred members of the Afro-American Society took over Straight Hall on the campus of Cornell University. Among their demands was the formation of an Africana center, where black students could learn about issues relevant to their race. In the midst of the occupation, some of the students armed themselves. After thirty-six hours, with their demands met, they exited the building with their rifles held high. "Oh, my God," cried an Associated Press photographer. "Look at those goddamned guns!" The next day, the image was plastered on the nation's newspapers.

The black studies movement was one of the major successes of the broader Black Power movement. By 1972, more than five hundred such programs were active on the nation's college campuses. Benefits were multifold: Black students learned about their people, past and present; they got to read and hear the perspectives of African Americans on traditional disciplines; and black students became enthusiastically engaged in education.

Moreover, the success of black studies encouraged other underserved groups to demand programs to meet their needs. In the 1970s and beyond, women's studies, Latino studies, and gay and lesbian studies emerged at schools nationwide.

Through the force of Black Power, diversity flowered on college campuses. In addition, it encouraged black Americans to sing, dance, write, talk, and dress in ways they never had before.

A black model with an afro, a hairstyle that became popular in the 1960s
and a fashion statement for the "black is beautiful" movement

CHAPTER 5

"I'M BLACK AND I'M PROUD"

One day in 1956, Mildred McCain got a talking-to by her black female teacher at their segregated school in Savannah, Georgia. "Mildred," the teacher informed her, "you are ugly. You have nappy hair and big lips, and you are black."

Prior to the civil rights and Black Power movements, the self-esteem of many black Americans was tragically low. White segregationists largely succeeded in denying black citizens not only their human rights but also their feelings of self-worth. In the South, many whites addressed black males not with their names but with the generic *boy* or *uncle*. Moreover, they derided them with such epithets as *coon*, *jigaboo*, *darkie*, and *nigger*.

Black children grew up hearing that their people were stupid and lazy, that they couldn't control their sexual urges or other impulses. Whites created caricatures of black people that made whites chuckle and blacks hang their heads. One early-1900s postcard, typical of the era, portrayed a black man with a huge mouth and giant lips

Two Coons.

(PC 55427

Postcards that degraded blacks were popular in the early 1900s.

resting on the ground and eating a big wedge of watermelon. The caption said, "You can plainly see how miserable I am." The most racist of whites thought that blacks were subhuman, and that they shouldn't bother praying because God wasn't listening.

Of course, segregation itself was enough to make a black person feel two feet tall. Baseball legend Hank Aaron discussed how humiliated he was when white restaurant workers deliberately smashed the dishes his Negro League team ate off of. "If dogs had eaten off those plates, they'd have washed them," he wrote. Even Martin Luther King Jr. was tongue-tied and embarrassed when he had to tell his daughter that she couldn't go to the Funtown amusement park because black people weren't allowed there.

Black militants such as Stokely Carmichael had spent their lives witnessing such humiliation, and they were sick of it. Known for "telling it like it is," Carmichael confronted the issue directly at Garfield High School in Seattle, Washington, on April 19, 1967:

[T]he most insidious things they could have done to us is to make us believe as a people that we are ugly. The criteria for beauty in this society is set by white folk. In the books you read, in the television programs you see, the movies, the magazines, and the newspaper. If she's beautiful, she's got a thin nose, thin lips, stringy hair, and white skin—and that's beauty. And they believe in that beauty so much that our women run around day and night bathing in beauty cream from morning to night.

They have got us believing that so that all these young men go out and process their hair so they can have straight hair to look beautiful. I hope you can take the truth, because they mesmerized our women's minds so that they process their hair every Friday night. And the rest of them get their fifty dollars and buy wigs. We have to as a people gather strength to stand up on our feet and say, 'Our noses are broad, our lips are thick, our hair is nappy—we are black and beautiful! Black and beautiful!'

While many people equate Black Power with fist-pumping militancy, the movement was far more complex and multifaceted. There were "softer" sides of the movement, those that encouraged black Americans to express themselves and feel good about who they were. The Black Power movement's sub-movements included the "black is beautiful" movement, the black pride movement, and the black arts movement.

The "black is beautiful" ethos may be the most important thing to arise from the Black Power movement. In what academics call internalized racism, many black Americans truly felt ugly and inferior because of the standard of beauty that whites had established. Many black Americans believed that light-skinned blacks were more attractive than those with dark skin, and they purchased creams designed to lighten their skin. Up through the mid-1900s, blacks in large cities held "paper bag parties." Only those with skin lighter than a paper bag were allowed to attend.

But attitudes dramatically changed when Black Power activists brought the issue to the fore. "Go home and tell your daughters they're beautiful," Carmichael said. Black Americans began wearing "Black Is Beautiful" buttons, and "Black is beautiful, baby!" became a popular catchphrase.

African Americans not only tossed their lightening creams and hot irons into the trash can, but they let their natural hair grow long. The large Afro, for both men and women, became a personal and cultural statement. Those who wore them seemed to say, "I am black, and I am proud of it." Angela Davis, a prominent black activist and feminist of the era, wore a large Afro. Not surprisingly, whites sometimes derided this symbol of black pride. Baseball fans used to laugh at outfielder Oscar Gamble, whose cap could barely contain the Afro beneath it.

In general, however, mainstream America began to accept the concept that "black is beautiful." In 1968, the editors of *Ladies' Home Journal* put dark-skinned model Naomi Sims on the cover of their November issue. The *New York Times* called it "a consummate moment of the Black is Beautiful movement."

Clothing also played a role in the "black is beautiful" and black pride movements. The more socially conscious blacks cast aside their conservative outfits and donned African-style clothing. Men wore long, loose-fitting, colorful, patterned shirts called dashikis as well as round, brimless, flattop caps known as kufis. Women also wore the garments of Africa with pride, including head cloths and long, patterned skirts.

Many black Americans felt a euphoric feeling of liberation during this period. According to *Ebony* magazine, some blacks even "adopted a Blacker-than-thou attitude. Many Blacks who had been embarrassed by Black styles in speech, food, dress and music now rushed to incorporate them as part of their unique identity."

"Black is beautiful" walked hand-in-hand with the black pride movement. While the former largely had to do with physical appearance, "black pride" referred to loving one's inner self, one's culture, one's heritage. Singer James Brown summed it up with the title of his 1968 hit: "Say It Loud—I'm Black and I'm Proud." In this funk song,

Naomi Sims, the daughter of a Pittsburgh maintenance worker, walks down Fifth Avenue in New York City on the way to a modeling assignment on June 23, 1969.

Brown calls out, "Say it loud," to which a group of children reply, "I'm black and I'm proud!" The song, which was No. 1 on the R&B singles chart for six weeks, became an anthem of the Black Power movement.

By the late 1960s, the lessons of Black Power teachers, lecturers, authors, and reporters were hitting home. In city neighborhoods and on college campuses, black pride was in the air. Black men and women called each other "brother" and "sister," even if they were meeting for the very first time. Young blacks greeted each other with a pumped-fist gesture—another sign of brotherhood.

The rise of black studies programs in the late 1960s reflected black Americans' surging interest in their heritage and culture. Many began to learn Swahili, a language spoken in nearly a dozen countries in Africa. Maulana Karenga, founder of the black nationalist United Slaves, explained why his people chose Swahili as opposed to some other African language. "We wanted to escape Western culture and tribalism, both," he said. "Swahili is not a tribal language—it represents a collective effort, and our group does, too."

Some black Americans "escaped Western culture" by changing their names. If a black man in the 1960s was named James Johnson, that meant that he had descended from a slave who had been given slave master Johnson's last name. Many black nationalists no longer wanted to be known by their slave names, and instead they chose Swahili, Hausa, Yoruba, or Arabic names. Hausa is the language of Chad, an African nation, and Yoruba is a dialect of West Africa. Many Black Muslims chose Arabic names, such as Cassius Clay becoming Muhammad Ali. Before the 1960s were over, Stokely Carmichael changed his name to Kwame Toure in honor of two African leaders with whom he associated.

Even the term used to describe black Americans was changed. Although Martin Luther King Jr. and many others still used the word *Negro*, many in the civil rights and Black Power movements objected to the term. They did not like its long, sad association with slavery, segregation, and discrimination. Activists preferred the term *black*, although its capitalization became an issue. Since *white*, when referring to Caucasians, had always been lower case, the mainstream media lowercased *black*. But Black Power activists cared little for grammatical niceties. *Black* with a capital *B* carried more weight than *black*, and it also contributed to stronger cultural identity, so they capitalized the term in most of their literature. *Afro-American* was used as a formal reference in the 1970s before falling out of vogue. The term *African American* (with or without a hyphen) emerged in the 1980s.

To those of the black pride movement, no meal tasted as good as "soul food." In 1962, black nationalist Amiri Baraka had been offended by an article that stated that black Americans had no cuisine of their own—that they simply had adopted the cuisine of the South. So Baraka penned an essay entitled "Soul Food" in which he listed foods that were distinctive to black culture:

> Hoppin' John (black-eyed peas and rice); hushpuppies (crusty corn meal bread cooked in fish grease and best with fried fish, especially fried salt fish, which ought to soak overnight unless you're over 50 and can't take all that salt); hoecake (pan cake); buttermilk biscuits and pancakes; fatback, i.e., streak'alean-streak'afat; dumplings; neck bones; knuckles, both good for seasoning lima or string beans; okra; pork chops; grits, eggs and sausage; pancakes with Alaga syrup; a chicken wing on a piece of greasy bread; a piece of barbecue hot enough to make you whistle; and small sweet potato pies.

In the 1960s, soul food came into vogue as a source of cultural pride. Black families didn't just gather to eat on Sunday afternoons; they embraced their heritage, which strengthened family bonds. Many soul food restaurants opened in the 1960s and 1970s, including such famous establishments as Sylvia's in Harlem and Edna's Restaurant in Chicago.

Soul music, a distinctively black genre, surged in popularity in the 1960s. Performers sang "from the soul," with their voices capturing the pain, anguish, and elation of the black experience. "I think what happened in the 1960s, with the advent of the Civil Rights Movement, blacks began to look down on blues as being too passive and rock 'n' roll as being too happy," said Tim Moore, communications director for the Rock and Roll Hall of Fame and Museum. "So we moved on to a more soulful music, and left whites with rock music."

Soul singers included such legends as Ray Charles, Al Green, Marvin Gaye, Lou Rawls, and Otis Redding. But the "Queen of Soul" was Aretha Franklin, who took the nation by storm with her 1967 album *I Never Loved a Man the Way I Loved You*. "Aretha's music," said soul musician Bobby Taylor, "makes you sweaty, gives you a chill, makes you want to stomp your feet."

Franklin's musical cries resonated with the powerful emotions and feelings of liberation that black Americans were experiencing in the late 1960s. Her hit songs "Respect" (1967) and "Think" (1968) served as anthems for African American women.

Just like civil rights activists had their "Freedom Songs" (such as "We Shall Overcome" and "Keep Your Eyes on the Prize"), Black Power proponents created music for their movement. The two-disc compilation album *Black Power: Music of a Revolution* provides a sampling of the artists and songs of the era. Tracks include those by the Chi-Lites ("Give More Power to the People"), Hank Ballard ("Blackenized"), the Temptations ("Message from a Black Man"), the Staple Singers ("Respect Yourself"), Nina Simone ("To Be Young, Gifted and Black"), and Gil Scott-Heron ("The Revolution Will Not Be Televised").

Of course, Black Power books had an impact on society. *The Autobiography of Malcolm X* (1965) became a sort of bible of the movement, selling 6 million copies by 1977. The aforementioned *Soul on Ice*, a collection of essays by Eldridge Cleaver, was another must-read of movement activists. *Soledad Brother: The Prison Letters of George Jackson* (1970) was a poignant book that made readers aware of the injustices of the judicial system.

Ray Charles with Aretha Franklin during a concert in February 1971

Sam Greenlee's *The Spook Who Sat by the Door* (1969) was among the unique novels of the period. Dan Freeman, the novel's hero, becomes the first African American to graduate from the CIA training corps. While pretending to be a do-good social worker in Chicago, he uses his CIA training techniques to convert black gang members into militant revolutionaries. The novel served as fantasy fulfillment for dispossessed black youth.

One Black Power activist even created a day of celebration. In the mid-1960s, black nationalists had vented their frustration that no black holiday existed. Declared Basir Mchawi, "It's time that we as Black People with Black families put down crazy cracker [a derisive word for white] celebrations for something that is for us. Think about it: Easter, Thanksgiving, Passover, Chanukah, X-Mas, Columbus, George Washington, Independence Day, on and on. Zillion of white holidays and lily-white images—but nothing for us."

In 1966, Maulana Karenga answered the call. He created Kwanzaa as a way for black families to reclaim the best traditions of African culture. The holiday, which is celebrated from December 26 to January 1, observes a set of seven principles called the Nguzo Saba. These principles, which are celebrated one day at a time, include unity, self-determination, collective work and responsibility, cooperative economics, purpose, creativity, and faith.

A family celebrating Kwanzaa

The holiday took hold during the Black Power era, and today it is celebrated by millions of people in the United States and other countries. Schools and communities that embrace multiculturalism accept Kwanzaa as one of the three major December holidays, along with Christmas and Chanukah.

The black pride movement stretched to all facets of society, including, according to Amistad Digital Resource, "black-oriented neighborhood schools, cultural centers, civic associations, and agencies that preached black self-reliance, self-respect, and a rejection of racial assimilation into the white world."

Like the Hippie movement, the black pride movement became so popular that corporations tried to capitalize on it. For example, Mattel launched the black Christie doll, as Barbie's friend, in 1968. By the 1970s, every major doll company would have a black doll on the market. Even the "black Santa Claus" and "black Jesus" became popular. Many whites found portrayals of a black Jesus as preposterous and blasphemous, but blacks countered that Jesus—who was from the Middle East—had been portrayed as white for centuries.

In 1968, NBC premiered the sitcom *Julia*, in which African American Diahann Carroll played a nurse who was a single mom. Although the show was ground breaking in that it featured a black woman in a lead role, critics complained that the show was safe and unrealistic in its dealing with black issues. It was obvious, they said, that NBC didn't want to alienate white viewers, who comprised the vast majority of their television audience. Carroll herself said in 1968, "At the moment we're presenting the white Negro. And he has very little Negro-ness."

When it came to films, Hollywood didn't have to worry about appeasing white audiences. Producers could turn a profit making films exclusively for black Americans. The result was the infamous "blaxploitation" (black exploitation) films of the early 1970s.

The genre began in 1971 when African American Melvin Van Peebles produced, directed, and scored the low-budget independent film *Sweet Sweetback's Baadasssss Song*. The plot, which involved a hero on the run from white authority, resonated with the black revolutionary spirit of the times—so much so that it was championed by Black Panthers co-founder Huey Newton.

The success of *Sweetback*, which topped $4 million at the box office, inspired the large, white-dominated Hollywood production companies to jump on the bandwagon. They produced their own films with militant or just simply violent black protagonists, and then screened them in black communities, exploiting the Black Power spirit of the times for their financial gain.

Blaxploitation films were filled with immoral characters and sordid situations. Violence, sex, prostitutes, pimps, and drugs were running themes, and they typically featured a black man (or woman) using a gun to get revenge. Some, such as the Gordon Parks films *Shaft* and *Super Fly*, became famous, while others, such as *Blacula* and *Blackenstein*, were just ridiculous. In general, the NAACP and socially conscious African Americans condemned Hollywood for rerouting the Black Power movement into films that furthered black stereotypes, to the detriment of the black race.

The literature and films (at least the finer ones) of the era were a part of the black arts movement (BAM), which Larry Neal defined in a 1968 essay as the "aesthetic and spiritual sister of the Black Power concept." Leaders of this artistic movement encouraged self-expression, which in itself was liberating. Like the Harlem Renaissance of the 1920s and 1930s, black artistic expression flourished during this period. Black arts meant everything from painting, sculpting, dancing, and playing music to writing plays, novels, and poetry—all of which reflected the black experience. "Blacks gave the example that you don't have to assimilate," said Ishmael Reed, a novelist and poet of the era. "You could do your own thing, get into your own background, your own history, your own tradition and your own culture."

Black artists were so empowered during the era that they commercialized their efforts. They opened publishing houses, magazines, art houses, and dance theaters so that the works of a few could be enjoyed by the masses. In 1969, Arthur Mitchell and Karel Shook formed the Dance Theatre of Harlem. At first, their dancing students practiced in a garage and performed at local schools, but within a few years they were touring the world.

In 1967, Haki R. Madhubuti invested the $400 that he had received for a poetry reading to buy a mimeograph machine. From his basement apartment in Chicago, he produced the first publications of his new company, Third World Press. The company went on to publish the works of powerful writers Amiri Baraka, Gwendolyn Brooks, and others and eventually grew into a multimillion-dollar enterprise.

Some of the black women writers of the day introduced readers to the rarely discussed topic of black feminism. Black feminists believed that both the black liberation movements and the women's movement (which emerged in the late 1960s) ignored issues specific to black women. Within the Black Power movement, black feminists believed, women were expected to play subservient roles. Black activist Elaine Brown recalled what the unwritten rules were in the early days of the Black Power movement: "Sisters . . . did not challenge Brothers. Sisters . . . stood behind their black men, supported their men, and respected them."

In general, black men felt that the concept of them being oppressors of black women was irrelevant or nonsensical because their whole race was being oppressed by whites. Meanwhile, white feminists made a similar argument: Race was not that relevant to the women's movement because all women were oppressed. Yet the leadership of the women's movement was nearly all white, as were the faculty of women's studies departments. Colleges and universities lacked classes devoted to black women's studies.

Finally, in 1973, two organizations emerged: the National Black Feminist Organization and Black Women Organized for Action. A year later, the Combahee River Collective was formed to address the issues of black lesbians, a group that battled racial, gender, and sexual-orientation discrimination.

To appreciate the enormous advances of the black pride movement, one can compare news footage of the Selma, Alabama, protests of January 1965 to film of the all-black 1975 play *The Wiz*. Selma protesters, in conservative dress and hairstyles, waited patiently in line in a nerve-racking attempt to register to vote. Many had their heads bowed or shoulders slumped as Sheriff Jim Clark and his deputies patrolled the sidewalks. Fast-forward ten years to the musical *The Wiz*, an African American take on the classic movie *The Wizard of Oz*.

The Broadway smash was a vibrant explosion of color and song, with distinctively black writing, acting, dancing, music, and artwork. "What made 'The Wiz' surprisingly moving . . . was that its creators **81**

Diana Ross (center) as Dorothy, Michael Jackson (right)
as Scarecrow, and Nipsey Russell as Tinman perform
during the filming of the musical *The Wiz* in New York.

found a connection between Baum's Kansas fantasy and the pride of urban black Americans," wrote Frank Rich of the *New York Times*. "When Glinda, the good witch, musically instructed Dorothy to believe in herself, she seemed to be delivering a broader inspirational message. The Wiz . . . had something to say, and it said it with verve and integrity."

If any "black revolution" took place in the late 1960s, it was a cultural one, thanks to the power of the black pride movement.

A mural of John F. Kennedy and
Martin Luther King Jr. in Chicago, Illinois

CHAPTER 6

BACKLASH AND PROGRESS

Martin Luther King Jr. had gotten into a pillow fight with his buddies at the Lorraine Motel in Memphis, Tennessee, on April 4, 1968, before getting ready for dinner. At one point, he walked onto the balcony and breathed in the chilly air.

"You think I need a coat?" he asked.

"Yeah, it's pretty cool and you've had a cold," said his friends and colleagues, including Andrew Young and Ralph Abernathy.

Moments later, King dropped to the balcony floor, the victim of an assassin's bullet. Abernathy lay with King as he slowly lost consciousness. "Oh God," cried Young. "Oh God, Ralph, it is over."

"Don't you say that, Andy," Abernathy shot back angrily. "Don't you say that. It is not over." But for all intents and purposes, the civil rights movement that King had led for thirteen years died with him on that tragic day in Memphis. Abernathy had been a solid lieutenant in the movement, but he did not possess the charisma and leadership qualities of Dr. King. Nobody did.

Black Power and revolutionary rhetoric, it seemed, was all that remained of the movement. But in the aftermath of the assassination, such militancy seemed only to hurt the cause, not help it.

When word of King's death reached the masses, black citizens took to the streets in anger. In a week unlike any other in American history, violence erupted in more than 120 American cities. In Detroit, 378 fires were reported and more than 1,400 people were arrested. In Chicago, two days of rioting led to nine deaths and 2,500 arrests. Chicago mayor Richard Daley ordered his police force to shoot to kill arsonists and shoot to maim looters. Across the strife-ridden nation, forty-six people were killed and some 3,000 were injured.

Two months later, presidential candidate Robert F. Kennedy, a friend of the movement, was assassinated in Los Angeles by a Palestinian immigrant. After King's death, black Americans had held out hope that at least Kennedy—as the possible next president—would facilitate the black agenda. But with Kennedy gone, hope seemed to vanish. Writing in the magazine *Ramparts*, Eldridge Cleaver declared, "Now there is only the gun and the bomb, dynamite and the knife, and they will be used liberally. . . . America will bleed. America will suffer."

Stokely Carmichael also felt it was time for a racial showdown. He asked black people to "stand up on our feet and die like men. If that's our only act of manhood, then goddam it we're going to die." Such proclamations were Black Power at its most dangerous. Many white Americans felt the pain of King's death, but at the same time they cringed at the violent Black Power rhetoric and the post-assassination riots—which erupted just months after the many deadly uprisings in the summer of 1967. Conservative Americans, who were also bothered by the angry antiwar protests on campus ("Hey, hey, LBJ, how many kids did you kill today?" was a popular student chant), were running low on empathy.

With President Johnson deciding that he would not seek reelection, the 1968 presidential race came down to Democratic vice president Hubert Humphrey and Republican Richard Nixon, the conservative vice president under Dwight Eisenhower back in the 1950s.

Richard Nixon, the thirty-seventh president of the United States

African Americans overwhelmingly supported Humphrey, who had earned the nickname "Happy Warrior" for his enthusiastic crusades for civil rights and social welfare programs dating back to the 1940s.

Nixon, meanwhile, hoped to prevent the presidential election of a third straight liberal Democrat. A conservative by nature, as well as an opportunist, Nixon sided with the majority of Americans—those who were not comfortable with the antiwar protesters, counterculture Hippies, and black militants. Running on a platform of "law and or-der," Nixon said he would answer to the "forgotten majority—the non-shouters and the nondemonstrators, the millions who ask principally to go their own way in decency and dignity."

The election was close, with Nixon garnering 31.8 million votes to Humphrey's 31.3 million but winning the electoral vote 301 to 191. What made southern blacks especially uneasy was that Independent candidate George Wallace—the famed segregationist governor of Alabama—won five southern states. Wallace's running mate was Curtis LeMay, the highly hawkish general who had commanded controversial firebombing attacks on sixty-four Japanese cities during World War II and had advised President Kennedy to attack Cuba during the 1962 missile crisis.

Nixon and his anti-militant vice president, Spiro Agnew, may have been better than Wallace/Lemay, blacks reasoned, but his administration would be no friend of the civil rights movement—let alone the Black Power movement.

As for the Black Panthers, everything seemed to be happening at once. In late 1968, the Party boasted chapters in twenty-five cities, with membership in excess of a thousand. Party member Eldridge Cleaver even ran for president in 1968, garnering nearly 36,571 votes as the candidate for the Peace and Freedom Party. That same month, Panthers co-founder Bobby Seale announced the establishment of community service programs, including several free health clinics, as well as the deliverance of free breakfasts to poor black children.

Despite these worthwhile programs, FBI director J. Edgar Hoover was out to destroy the Panthers. On August 25, 1967, Hoover had begun a counterintelligence program (COINTELPRO) designed to, according to his confidential memo to FBI offices, "expose, disrupt, misdirect, discredit, or otherwise neutralize the activities of black nationalist, hate-type organizations and groupings, their leadership, spokesmen, membership, and supporters, and to counter their propensity for violence and civil disorder."

One of Hoover's goals was to prevent the rise of a black "messiah." Besides the late Malcolm X, he listed three black leaders with such potential: King, Carmichael, and Nation of Islam leader Elijah Muhammad. At first, the Panthers were not on Hoover's list of "black nationalist, hate-type organizations." The SNCC, the Nation of Islam, and King's nonviolent SCLC were. But in September 1968, Hoover called the Black Panther Party "the greatest threat to the internal security of the country." According to *Voices of Freedom*, "In all, of the 295 COINTELPRO actions against black groups, 233 targeted the Panthers."

Although progressives, including John and Robert Kennedy, had been at odds with Hoover, Nixon and the FBI chief shared a similar disdain for political dissidents. In fact, Nixon ordered the FBI to spy on the Panthers and other organizations. These COINTELPRO "actions" included smear campaigns, such as the infamous coloring book case. The FBI disseminated the Black Panthers Coloring Book, claiming it was a sordid example of the party's indoctrination of children. The book featured revolting pictures, such as a little boy in an Afro shooting two pigs dressed in police uniforms. In reality, the Panthers neither produced nor condoned the coloring book, but the FBI made people believe that they had.

THE PIG IS AFRAID OF BLACK CHILDREN BECAUSE THEY ARE BRAVE WARRIORS

An illustration from the dubious Black Panthers Coloring Book showing a black boy shooting two policemen portrayed as pigs in uniforms

Working closely with the FBI, police began to crack down on the Panthers in 1969. They raided party headquarters and the homes of Panther leaders in multiple cities, including a deadly raid in Chicago on December 4, 1969. According to the police, more than a dozen officers fired on Panthers Fred Hampton and Mark Clark—killing them—because Hampton and Clark had fired first. "We wholeheartedly commend the police officers' bravery, their remarkable restraint and discipline in the face of this vicious Black Panther attack," stated Cook County state's attorney Edward V. Hanrahan. Yet evidence showed that Hampton and Clark had been sleeping at the time of the predawn raid, and that Hampton had been drugged by an FBI informant. Thirteen years later, survivors of the deceased would receive $1.85 million in compensation from the city, county, and federal government.

Also in 1969, authorities charged twenty-one Panthers with arson, conspiracy (to blow up buildings), and attempted murder. The trial did not take place until 1971, but due to lack of evidence, the jury quickly acquitted those who stood trial. To a large extent, the FBI and police were succeeding in destroying the Panthers. Members felt the pressure from all angles. "[I]t's like the Panthers were all of a sudden thrust into the forefront of being the alternative [to King's movement]," said Kathleen Neal Cleaver, the wife of Eldridge Cleaver, "and maybe [they] weren't anticipating as much attention as they got—neither the media attention nor the police repression. 'Cause they sort of went hand in hand. The more repression, the more media attention; the more media attention, the more repression."

In 1970, Huey Newton was released from prison after his manslaughter charge was reversed on appeal. With his party in disarray, he tried to de-emphasize police confrontations and focus on helpful programs: free breakfasts, free health clinics, liberation schools, and petition campaigns for community control of police. Nevertheless, the Panthers became less and less of a force. Seale lost a mayoral race in Oakland in 1973, and Newton moved to Cuba the following year. Elaine Brown served ably as chairperson from 1974 to 1977, expanding community service programs, but the organization disbanded in 1982.

Other Black Power organizations also ran out of steam. After H. Rap Brown resigned from the SNCC in 1968 after being indicted for starting the Cambridge, Maryland, riot, the group dropped out of the national spotlight. The Republic of New Afrika (RNA), which had proposed a black nation in the South, was a COINTELPRO target. In a dramatic confrontation in August 1971, the FBI and Jackson police stormed the RNA government residence with tear gas, arms, and a tank. Fighting back, RNA members killed Jackson police officer William Skinner. The case went to trial, and eight RNA members were convicted and sentenced to life in prison.

The Congress of Racial Equality (CORE), a prominent civil rights organization since 1942, rode the tide of the times. Once at the forefront of the civil rights movement (with the Freedom Rides, March on Washington, and Freedom Summer), CORE supported the Black Power movement until 1968, when the group—under new national chairman Roy Innis—surprisingly supported Richard Nixon's presidential campaign. CORE has been a politically conservative organization ever since.

Many Americans feel that the Black Liberation Army (BLA), a loosely organized entity comprised of some former Black Panthers, was little more than a terrorist organization. Instead of accepting that authorities had "won the war" with black nationalist groups like the Panthers, BLA members went underground and fought back. One of their stated missions was to "take up arms for the liberation and self-determination of black people in the United States."

Dozens of violent acts, from arson and bombings to kidnapping and murder, were linked to members of the BLA. In fact, BLA members were blamed for the killings of some thirteen police officers. In 1971, for example, five men were arrested for the shooting deaths of two New York City police officers. Also that year, the BLA was blamed for the murder of a San Francisco officer as he sat at his desk.

Although the Black Liberation Army was an exceptionally radical organization—not at all like the more mainstream Black Power groups—many Americans still blamed the Black Power philosophy for birthing the BLA. After all, it was Malcolm X who had insisted on "any means necessary" to achieve racial justice, and armed resistance was a running theme in Black Power rhetoric.

While militant Black Power organizations died out in the early 1970s, the idea of Black Power—in terms of political and economic black empowerment—remained strong. In 1969, the African American members of Congress formed the Congressional Black Caucus so they could address black issues together. In 1971, they presented a list of sixty recommendations to President Nixon. When they felt that he did not take the issues seriously enough, the Caucus members boycotted his State of the Union address. Ever since, the Caucus has made its presence felt on Capitol Hill.

In 1972, some 8,000 African Americans gathered in Gary, Indiana, for the National Black Political Convention. Delegates denounced the concept of "busing"—in which some black students were bused to better white schools and white students were bused to black schools—and instead called for black Americans to improve their own schools and communities. They had other ideas as well, such as establishing a national network of community health centers.

Students at Horace Mann Junior High School in Little Rock, Arkansas, line up to board a school bus that will take them from the predominantly black East Side to their homes on the West Side in 1971.

Although most of their goals were out of reach, the delegates showed that the spirit of black Americans was still strong—despite the murder of King and the FBI crackdowns. "Black politics demands new vision, new hope and new definitions of the possible," the convention's agenda stated. "Our time has come. These things are necessary. All things are possible."

For black Americans in the 1970s, the news was mixed. Conditions definitely improved for blacks in the South, as the Civil Rights Act of 1964 and Voting Rights Act of 1965 had pretty much killed off Jim Crow. In Mississippi, the number of registered black voters had jumped from 6.7 percent in 1964 to 59 percent in 1968. By 1970, 711 African Americans held elected positions in the eleven southern states, nearly ten times more than in 1965.

Overall in the U.S., more and more African Americans were graduating high school and college, which would lead to a growing black middle class in subsequent years. In northern cities, antidiscrimination laws allowed more blacks to land government jobs, including those on the police force. The legacy of the Black Power movement paid off on election days, as black citizens turned out in force to vote for black candidates. African Americans won mayoral races in Newark (Kenneth Gibson) in 1970 and Atlanta (Maynard Jackson), Detroit (Coleman Young), and Los Angeles (Tom Bradley) in 1973. A year later, Walter E. Washington became the mayor of Washington, DC.

While Black Power assertiveness had helped blacks gain more political control in their cities, it contributed to a tragic fallout effect: "white flight." White flight, which began after World War II, refers to white people moving out of the big cities and into the suburbs. Many reasons contributed to this phenomenon, including the construction of millions of lovely homes in pleasant suburban neighborhoods. Moreover, the widespread construction of freeways in the 1950s and beyond allowed workers to commute from the suburbs to downtown offices in no time. The appeal of this "American dream" lifestyle attracted people to the suburbs.

That said, black militancy also facilitated white flight. After the horrific riots of 1967 and April 1968, and images of black militancy and violence on the evening news, whites were eager to flee their urban communities. In some metropolitan areas, the white flight was dramatic. At South Shore High School in Chicago, the black student population jumped from 1.5 percent in 1963 to 73 percent in 1968.

According to historian Jeffrey Ogbonna Green Ogbar, it wasn't just black violence but changing black attitudes that prompted whites to leave. Regarding South Shore High, he wrote, "White students who had engaged in humiliating attacks against black students for years were on the defensive as black militancy swept the student body." Discussing black students in general, Ogbar wrote, "The fights, short tempers, and intolerance for any perceived infraction against black humanity were pervasive among young blacks. They represented a clear rejection of the general ethos of peace from the civil rights movement. . . . They unequivocally rejected the stereotypes of the perennially happy and slow-to-anger Negro." In addition, as more and more black candidates were elected to office in the 1970s—with promises to improve conditions for African Americans in their cities—whites felt increasingly "outnumbered." All of these conditions accelerated the process of white flight.

Detroit epitomized the phenomenon of white flight and its tragic results. In the Motor City, the white population dropped from 71 percent in 1960 to 56 in 1970 to 36 in 1980 to 22 in 1990. Conversely, the black population over that period rose from 29 percent to 44, 64, and 78. Over that period, the city fell steadily and dramatically into decline. While many Michiganders blamed Mayor Coleman Young for the city's failings, loss of tax revenue was a major problem. When the wealthier Detroiters moved to the suburbs, they no longer paid property taxes to the city government, nor were they around to buy products at local stores or dine at local restaurants, meaning the city's sales tax revenue plummeted.

The white population of Detroit fell from 839,000 in 1970 to 421,000 in 1980. As whites fled and the overall population dropped, many small businesses in the city closed shop. As the city continued to deteriorate—and crime inevitably increased—many suburbanites no longer wanted to even venture into the city, either for work or pleasure. Many big companies closed their downtown offices and opened in new suburban business communities, such as those in Troy. When the evening news would report on a black-on-white rape or shooting downtown, particularly during a major event such as the Fourth of July fireworks many whites would typically say, "That's it! I'm never going downtown again."

A deserted building in Detroit. Parts of the city became an urban wasteland as its population declined.

With declining property and sales tax revenue, and falling revenues from downtown businesses and downtown shoppers, Detroit fell into disarray. Many other big cities, such as Cleveland and Washington, DC, experienced similar misery, as did parts of Chicago (the South Side) and New York (most notably the Bronx). In these cities, unemployment and crime soared. Businesses barred their windows. Houses became abandoned, with lawns overgrown and windows boarded up. Drug use became rampant, especially the use of crack cocaine in the 1980s and 1990s. The federal government responded with stiff mandatory sentencing for selling and possessing crack, resulting in the incarceration of huge numbers of black males. (The U.S. prison population increased by 700 percent from 1970 to 2005.)

In most big cities, despair ran high among African Americans. More and more black babies were born out of wedlock and in thousands of cases addicted to crack. Public housing projects were overcrowded and drug-infested. Public schools became "failure factories." Schools were underfunded, with high incidences of gang involvement and drug use in the junior highs and high schools. Few good teachers wanted to work in such conditions, and high school dropout rates among black males exceeded 50 percent in some cities. The large number of single mothers, who had to work full-time, found child-raising extremely challenging—especially if gangs and drugs were rampant in their communities.

Of course, some African Americans did "escape" the ghettos. Those who graduated college and landed good jobs moved to nice pockets of the city or to mostly black suburbs, such as Southfield, Michigan, and Prince George's County, Maryland. But for most urban African Americans, moving to the suburbs was often rife with complications. In many cases, the housing was too expensive. Moreover, in many suburbs across the country, residents resisted the influx of African Americans. Nonblacks talked about how the crime rate would rise and property values would fall if blacks moved in. Blacks, meanwhile, were disinclined to move to communities in which they obviously weren't wanted. The black populations of most of America's nicest suburbs would remain infinitesimal.

Unlike the civil rights movement, which achieved its stated goals of dismantling Jim Crow segregation, the Black Power movement did not culminate in anything tangible. It just gradually dissipated, leaving it to historians—many years later—to try to evaluate it.

In the end, Black Power gave individuals a feeling of liberation. Black pride, "black is beautiful," and the black arts transformed oppression into self-expression. On a societal level, the movement empowered African Americans to stand up to police oppression and other forms of discrimination in urban areas. Yet it also led to many deadly riots as well as considerable backlash: the election of a law-and-order hardliner as president, FBI raids, and the facilitation of white flight, which greatly contributed to disastrous urban conditions.

"There were lots of mistakes and incredible flaws in what we did," summarized Ericka Huggins, a leader in the Black Panther Party, "but there were also many successful things, including community support and education programs as well as helping to change the way in which African American people think and speak about themselves. Sadly, however, there is still so much to be done."

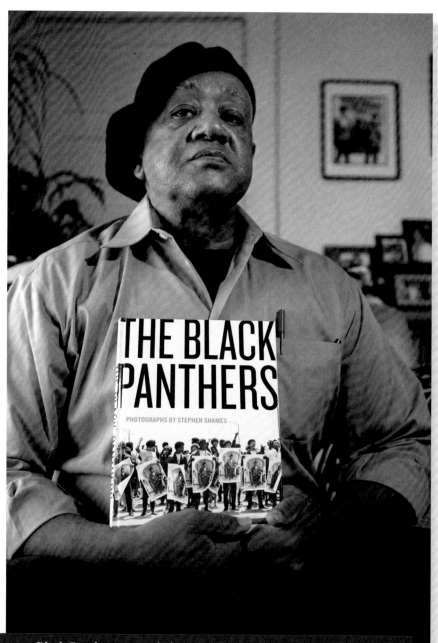

Former Black Panther national chairman Bobby Seale holds up a book about the Black Panther Party at his home in Oakland, California, in 2006.

CHAPTER 7

BLACK POWER TODAY

If you flip through the cable channels, you would think that black America is thriving. ESPN often has breaking news on the latest black star of the National Football League or National Basketball Association who signed for millions of dollars. African Americans, who comprise approximately 12 percent of the U.S. population, are amply represented in movies, television, and music. Since most Americans consider multiculturalism a good thing, advertisers frequently feature black Americans in their ads—often as members of the middle or upper middle classes. In addition, with a black family now in the White House, many think that we now live in a "post-racial" society.

But Barack Obama, LeBron James, Chris Rock, and Rihanna are not representative of black America. Overall, the condition of African Americans is considerably worse than that of white Americans, prompting calls for a new kind of "black power." Today's black leaders are not asking for armed insurrection or a separate black nation. Instead, they are urging African Americans to empower themselves and their communities while continuing to challenge racial injustice.

Although the black middle class has grown dramatically since the 1960s, great inequities still remain between white and black Americans. In 2006, the average (median) household income for whites in the United States was $50,673, compared to $31,969 for blacks. While 8.2 percent of non-Hispanic white Americans lived in poverty in 2007, 24.5 of blacks endured such conditions.

For black Americans, the troubling statistics never seem to end. For example, the typical African American is much less likely than a white person to graduate from a four-year college. This is due largely to the substandard public school systems in urban areas (where more than 80 percent of African Americans live) as well as the high cost of college education.

More startling, the average wealth (net worth) of a white household in the United States is roughly eight times greater than that of a black household. A key factor in this disparity dates back to the "white flight" era. A person who bought a suburban house in 1960 (and at the time, the suburbs were almost exclusively white) for, say, $25,000 could have sold it in the 1990s for hundreds of thousands of dollars. The home sellers could then pass that wealth to their children, who could use it for buying homes and/or investing in their children's education.

In 2009, the *Chicago Sun-Times* reported that the racial "health care gap kills 3,200 black Chicagoans a year—and the gap is growing." Dr. Steven Whitman of Chicago's Sinai Urban Health Institute said that African Americans in poor inner-city neighborhoods lacked access to quality health care, did not have enough parks and recreation areas, and had few healthy-food options due to a dearth of grocery stores in their communities. Many have complained that fast food restaurants, which are popular in lower-income communities largely because of low prices (a cheeseburger can cost less than an orange), contribute to high levels of child obesity in urban areas.

A popular perception among many Americans is that blacks are to blame for their continued low socioeconomic status. They say that anti-discrimination laws were passed in the 1960s (including the Fair Housing Act in 1968) and that blacks have even received an extra boost due to affirmative action programs. However, others counter that institutional discrimination still remains and is the main cause of racial inequalities.

One of the most glaring forms of institutional racism is in the field of education. On September 2, 2008, Chicago public school students boycotted their first day of classes and staged a protest at New Trier Township High School in the wealthy suburb of Northfield. Protesters pointed out that $15,000 was spent annually on each child at New Trier compared to $10,000 in Chicago—hardly an equal playing field. "It's totally separate and totally unequal," said Arne Duncan, chief executive of the Chicago school system who would become U.S. secretary of education in 2009. "The children of the rich get a different education than the children of the poor."

The nonprofit Education Trust estimated that in 2005 the average gap in annual per-pupil spending among high-income and low-income districts in the U.S. was $938.

Another alarming statistic comes from legal scholar Michelle Alexander in her 2010 book *The New Jim Crow: Mass Incarceration in the Age of Colorblindness*. She found that there are more black Americans under correctional control today than were enslaved in 1850. In 2008, the Pew Center on the States released a report stating that one in nine black men between the ages of twenty and thirty-four were incarcerated. Many have blamed the high rate on the stiff mandatory prison sentences created in response to the crack cocaine epidemic of the 1980s. Mere possession of crack, which has been prevalent in black communities, can result in a prison sentence. Most of the people in prison are incarcerated for nonviolent, drug-related crimes.

Laws created by the white majority that severely punish "black" crimes but are lenient on "white" (such as corporate) crimes is an example of the institutional racism that exists in the United States. So is harsher sentencing for blacks compared to whites who commit the same crimes; better funding for white parts of a city than for black neighborhoods; refusal of corporations to open grocery stores in inner cities, resulting in poor food options for African Americans; and **103** a disinterest by the white majority in resolving crises that face the poor, such as homelessness, dangerous neighborhoods, and inadequate health care.

The recent recession worsened the condition of African Americans. While white Americans suffered considerably during the economic crisis, with unemployment rising 4.5 percentage points (4.2 to 8.7) from 2007 to January 2010, African Americans bore a heavier burden, with a 7.4 percent rise in unemployment over that same period (9.1 to 16.5). Moreover, the national foreclosure crisis—in which millions of Americans lost their homes because they could no longer afford to pay the mortgage—hit African Americans especially hard.

Many black leaders have concluded that the social programs of former liberal administrations—such as large public housing projects and the welfare system—have not helped African Americans rise to a higher economic level. Many black activists agree that the true path to prosperity is twofold: 1) continue to fight to remove racial injustice and 2) empower black individuals and communities. In a sense, these are modern equivalents to the civil rights movement and the Black Power movement.

The NAACP continues to lead the way in the fight for equal rights. One of the organization's recent battles was protecting the Voting Rights Act of 1965. Some right-wingers believe the act is no longer necessary because Americans have elected a black president. But NAACP president Benjamin Jealous stated that a great deal of voter discrimination and intimidation still exists, and that the act must remain intact to protect minorities' rights.

There are hundreds of organizations that address black issues. The National Urban League has been a leader in fighting for black employment, as has the Congressional Black Caucus. In its 2010 agenda, the Caucus called for better funding for education and job training, various ways to improve the economic conditions of African Americans, the elimination of health disparities, providing good housing options, strengthening civil rights and judicial reform, and addressing global poverty.

The Sentencing Project is a leading advocate of sentencing reform, and its efforts have borne fruit. The project still has a long way to go, because, as its Web site states, "one in three young black men is under control of the criminal justice system," "five million Americans can't vote because of felony convictions," and "thousands of women and children have lost welfare, education and housing benefits as the result of convictions for minor drug offenses."

While organizations such as the NAACP and the Caucus push government to rectify injustices, other black activists urge individuals and communities to "get their own house in order." In recent years, entertainer Bill Cosby has discussed the need for a better value system in African American communities. He is upset that 70 percent of African American babies are born out of wedlock, and in a 2004 speech he had plenty to say about parenting and personal responsibility: "I'm talking about these people who cry when their son is standing there in an

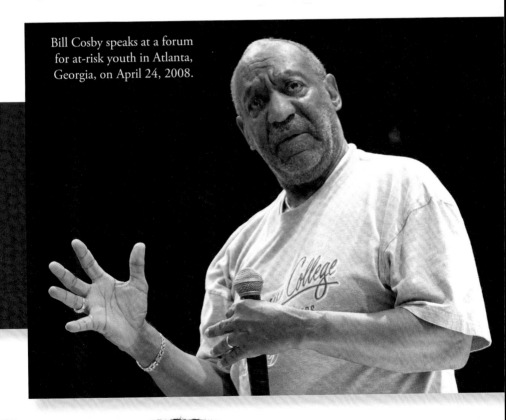

Bill Cosby speaks at a forum for at-risk youth in Atlanta, Georgia, on April 24, 2008.

orange [prison] jumpsuit. Where were you when he was two? Where were you when he was twelve? Where were you when he was eighteen, and how come you don't know he had a pistol?"

As for black urban youth, Cosby said, "It's cursing and calling each other nigga as they're walking up and down the street. They think they're hip. They can't read. They can't write. They're laughing and giggling, and they're going nowhere."

Cosby's words caused a firestorm of controversy within the black community. Some didn't like his patronizing tone, and others said he was making unfair generalizations. Others pointed to the many systemic issues as causing most of the problems in black society. In his 2005 book *Is Bill Cosby Right?*, noted black academic Michael Eric Dyson strongly challenged Cosby's assertions. As reviewer Keith A. Owens put it, "Dyson swings back with the counterargument that Cosby should pick on somebody his own size and stop beating up on the weakest, most traumatized and defenseless group of people among us."

During his presidential campaign in 2008, U.S. senator Barack Obama rekindled the controversy with remarks that were similar to Cosby's. In what was described as a tough-love speech, Obama told a crowd of supporters in Beaumont, Texas, to stop eating cold Popeye's chicken for breakfast. He added: "It's not good enough for you to say to your child, 'Do good in school,' and then when that child comes home, you got the TV set on, you got the radio on, you don't check their homework, there is not a book in the house, you've got the video game playing."

While both Cosby and Obama were heartily criticized (Jesse Jackson later accused Obama of talking down to black people), they in a sense were echoing the words of the Black Power era: African Americans need to step up and take control of their destinies.

President Barack Obama at the University of Minnesota on October 23, 2010

The Nation of Islam, an all-black religious organization, made a strong statement in that regard on October 16, 1995. In the famous Million Man March, hundreds of thousands of African American men gathered in Washington, DC, for a "day of atonement." They gathered to display their commitment to their families and to the black community, and to counteract the negative image of black men often portrayed in the media.

As in the Black Power era, many contemporary black nationalist groups currently exist on the fringes of society. The Southern Poverty Law Center lists close to a thousand "hate groups" active in the United States. Most of them are white nationalist groups, but the list also includes 113 black separatist groups. One of the organizations on the list is the New Black Panther Party, which is not affiliated with the original Black Panther Party.

In 1998, 2,000 black activists—including former members of Black Power groups, such as Angela Davis and Amiri Baraka—took part in the founding of the Black Radical Congress. Their fifteen-part "Freedom Agenda" listed ways in which they would try to eradicate injustice and improve the lives of African Americans. The Black Radical Congress vowed to struggle for the abolition of the death penalty, fight to abolish unwarranted incarceration, support the liberation of all oppressed people, and more. The Black Radical Congress, however, never became a major force.

In recent years, black leaders have grown increasingly frustrated. With the black unemployment rate in the midteens during the recession, many African Americans have fallen out of the middle class while the black poverty rate has gone up. Many good social programs have lost funding due to budget cuts. In New York City, Project U Turn had helped thousands of at-risk youth turn their lives around at a per-person cost that was only a small fraction of the cost of incarceration. However, their public funding was cut off in 2010.

The key to black success, most agree, is through quality education. But with state and local governments facing budget crises all over the country, many legislatures were trimming public school budgets. Some parents put their hopes in charter schools, which do not charge tuition and are run by a government agency, university, nonprofit organization, or corporation. Charter schools employ alternative teaching techniques and often have a more intense curriculum. There are more than 5,000 charter schools in the United States, and they are particularly popular in urban communities that have woeful public schools.

Not everyone believes that charter schools are better than public schools, but no one can deny the success of Geoffrey Canada and the Harlem Children's Zone (HCZ). Covering nearly a hundred blocks in Central Harlem, the HCZ teaches 1,200 children at the Promise Academy Charter School and also provides support to the children who attend public schools in the zone. The test scores of the Promise Academy students are extremely high, as is the rate of high schoolers going on to college.

The Harlem Children's Zone touts itself as "a unique, holistic approach to rebuilding a community so that its children can stay on track through college and go on to the job market. The goal is to create a 'tipping point' in the neighborhood so that children are surrounded by an enriching environment of college-oriented peers and supportive adults, a counterweight to 'the street' and a toxic popular culture that glorifies misogyny and anti-social behavior."

The Harlem Children's Zone is the type of self-sufficient, black-empowerment success story that the old Black Power activists dreamt about. Barack Obama was so impressed that, during his presidential campaign, he vowed to create Promise Neighborhoods based on the HCZ model in twenty other cities.

In a post-recession nation, African Americans could rise above if such alternative education programs are successful. Civil rights historian Todd Burroughs adds: "Education is still the best way out, but now it must be coupled with entrepreneurship. . . . Black Americans in the 21st century have to take the strength of their American ancestors who fought against slavery and Jim Crow and couple it with the same streetwise, survival-fueled innovation that pushed them to create billion-dollar entertainment genres, such as jazz and hip-hop."

The Harlem Children's Zone Promise Academy

Signs indicate that African Americans are indeed inclined to launch their own businesses. In 2003, a Marion Kaufman Foundation study found that blacks were 50 percent more likely than whites or Hispanics to start their own company. New small-business ventures have dropped off dramatically in recent years due to the recession. But in better times, aggressive entrepreneurship by African Americans could be a key to success. Dramatic advancements in education and business would be a winning combination—one certainly worthy of a Black Power salute.

A 1969 photo of a young man holding up a clenched
fist as a greeting and gesture of Black Power

TIMELINE

1962	Black militant Robert F. Williams publishes influential book *Negroes with Guns*.
1965	Stokely Carmichael of the Student Nonviolent Coordinating Committee (SNCC) helps found the Lowndes County Freedom Organization in Alabama; black insurrection in Watts section of Los Angeles leads to thirty-four deaths and some 4,000 arrests; *The Autobiography of Malcolm X* published.
1966	Militant activist Stokely Carmichael replaces non-violence advocate John Lewis as chairman of the SNCC; during speech in Greenwood, Mississippi, Carmichael inspires crowd with calls for "Black Power"; leaders of nonviolent civil rights movement, including Martin Luther King Jr., voice their reservations, and, in some cases, condemnation of Black Power; in Oakland, Bobby Seale and Huey Newton found Black Panther Party; black national-ist Maulana Karenga creates holiday Kwanzaa to help black families reclaim the best traditions of African culture.
1966-early 1970s	Interconnected black pride, "black is beautiful," and black arts movements flower throughout nation, characterized by use of *Black* instead of *Negro*, African clothing, the Afro, self-respect, and celebration of heritage.
1967	Thirty armed Black Panthers march into California Capitol building to voice their opposition to anti-gun bill; race riot in Detroit, forty-three die; rioting sweeps through Newark, New Jersey, twenty-six die; Newark Black Power Conference held three days after rioting ends; speech by black militant H. Rap Brown prompts rioting in Cambridge, Maryland; Black Panther Party co-founder Huey Newton arrested for death of Oakland police officer.
1967 and beyond	Black militancy and race riots facilitate "white flight" in many cities.

1968	Federally organized Kerner Report blames 1967 riots on poverty and discrimination as well as inferior schools, housing, and public services; prominent Black Panther Eldridge Cleaver publishes *Soul on Ice*, a collection of essays; the Republic of New Afrika, which calls for an all-black nation in the American South, produces its Declaration of Independence; Martin Luther King Jr. assassinated, triggering calls for armed revolution and rioting in more than 120 American cities over several days; black autoworkers in Detroit form Dodge Revolutionary Union Movement (DRUM), which will inspire other black unions; James Brown song "Say It Loud—I'm Black and I'm Proud" released; American sprinters Tommie Smith and John Carlos give Black Power salute on medal podium at Summer Olympics in Mexico City.
1969	Congressional Black Caucus formed; black studies movement heats up, with students demanding programs on numerous college campuses; FBI intensifies efforts to crack down on Black Panther Party and other black nationalist groups, resulting in numerous deadly confrontations in this year and beyond.
1970	The radical, militant Black Liberation Army forms; members will commit numerous violent acts, including the murder of police officers.
1971	Success of Melvin Van Peebles film *Sweet Sweetback's Baadasssss Song* indirectly sparks "blaxploitation" film genre.
1972	Some 8,000 black delegates attend National Black Political Convention in Gary, Indiana; with a law-and-order platform, Republican Richard Nixon defeats Democrat Hubert Humphrey in presidential election; Black Panther Eldridge Cleaver garners 36,571 votes as presidential candidate.
1973	National Black Feminist Organization and Black Women Organized for Action form.
1982	Black Panther Party disbands.

SOURCES

CHAPTER 1: A NEW KIND OF MOVEMENT

p. 9,   "Selma, Alabama, became . . ." Martin Luther King Jr., *A Testament of Hope* (New York: HarperCollins, 1990), 228.

p. 11,   "sit down together . . ." "Martin Luther King, Jr./'I Have a Dream,'" American Rhetoric: Top 100 Speeches, http://www.americanrhetoric.com/speeches/mlkihaveadream.htm.

p. 11,   "Some negroes have . . ." Josh Gottheimer, *Ripples of Hope: Great American Civil Rights Speeches* (New York: Basic Civitas Books, 2004), 297–298.

p. 12,   "The black panther . . ." Henry Hampton and Steve Fayer, *Voices of Freedom* (New York: Bantam Books, 1990), 277.

p. 13,   "A fundamental change . . ." Charles J. Hamilton Jr., "SNCC: Brass Tacks," The *Harvard Crimson*, http://www.thecrimson.com/article/1967/5/4/sncc-pat-a-student-non-violent-coordinating.

p. 13,   "The new Howard . . ." Ibid.

p. 15,   "the fiery orator . . ." "Mukasa Willie Ricks and the Voting Rights Act of 1965," Associated Content, http://www.associatedcontent.com/article/1208593/mukasa_willie_ricks_and_the_voting_pg2.html?cat=37.

p. 15,   "their speeches were . . ." Cleveland Sellers, *The River of No Return* (Jackson: University Press of Mississippi, 1990), 166.

p. 15,   "This is the . . ." Ibid., 166–167.

p. 17,   "At each interview . . ." Ibid., 168.

p. 17,   "staunch ally and . . ." Ibid., 169.

CHAPTER 2: WHAT EXACTLY WAS BLACK POWER?

p. 19,   "I have always . . ." "Deborah Rand," Civil Rights Movement Veterans, http://www.crmvet.org/vet/randd.htm.

p. 20,   "I've given up . . ." Gordon Parks, "Whip of Black Power," *Life*, May 19, 1967, 82.

p. 20,   "*For the last* . . ." Ibid.

p. 20,   "If America don't . . ." Therese Mulligan, *Bernie Boston* (Rochester, N.Y.: RIT Cary Graphic Arts Press, 2006), 13.

p. 23,   "The white man . . ." Parks, *Life*, 82.

p. 24,   "we had seen . . ." Huey P. Newton, et al., *The Huey P. Newton Reader* (New York: Seven Stories Press, 2002), 49.

CHAPTER 3: THE ROOTS OF BLACK POWER

p. 27,   "We didn't land . . ." "A ESC Tribute to Malcolm X," Ethnic Student Center, http://esc.as.wwu.edu/x/quotes.html.

p. 28,   "Everybody has asked . . ." "Three Speeches from Frederick Douglass: Examples of His Passion, Logic and Power," FrederickDouglass.org, http://www.frederickdouglass.org/speeches.

pp. 30-31,   "We want full . . ." "W. E. B. DuBois: Address to the Nation," Wake Forest University, http://www.wfu.edu/~zulick/341/niagara.html.

p. 32,   "Separate educational facilities . . ." "*Brown v. Board of Education*, 347 U.S. 483 (1954)," The National Center for Public Policy Research, http://www.nationalcenter.org/brown.html.

p. 32,	"issued a document . . ." "Our History," SCLC, http://sclcnational.org/core/item/page.aspx?s=25461.0.12.2607.
p. 35,	"The murder shocked . . ." "Kareem Abdul-Jabbar," Emmett Till Murder, http://www.emmetttillmurder.com/Jabbar.htm.
p. 35,	"When I first . . ." Michael T. Kaufman, "Stokely Carmichael, Rights Leader Who Coined 'Black Power,' Dies at 57," *New York Times*, November 16, 1998, http://www.nytimes.com/1998/11/16/us/stokely-carmichael-rights-leader-who-coined-black-power-dies-at-57.html.
p. 35,	"I've got vengeance . . ." Juan Williams, *Eyes on the Prize* (New York: Penguin Books, 1987), 240.
p. 36,	"Tonight the Negro . . ." Ibid., 219.
p. 37,	"has been tampered . . ." "Nation of Islam," Allaahuakbar.net, http://www.allaahuakbar.net/nation/nation_of_islam.htm.
p. 38,	"7. WE BELIEVE this . . ." "What We Believe," The Nation of Islam, http://www.noi.org/muslim_program.htm.
p. 39,	"quickly earned a . . ." Clayborne Carson, primary consultant, *Civil Rights Chronicle* (Lincolnwood, Ill.: Legacy Publishing, 2003), 263.
p. 39,	"Nobody can give . . ." "Malcolm X Quotes," Thinkexist.com, http://thinkexist.com/quotation/nobody_can_give_you_freedom-nobody_can_give_you/251191.html.
p. 39,	"Nonviolence is fine . . ." "Nonviolence Quotes," BrainyQuote, http://www.brainyquote.com/quotes/keywords/nonviolence.html.
p. 39,	"Be peaceful, be . . ." "Malcolm X Quotes," Thinkexist.com, http://thinkexist.com/quotation/be_peaceful-be_courteous-obey_the_law-respect/250988.html.
p. 39,	"by any means . . ." "Quotations," malcolm-x.org, http://www.malcolm-x.org/quotes.htm.
p. 40,	"The Negroes of . . ." James Baldwin, *The Price of the Ticket* (New York: Macmillan, 1985), 371.
p. 40,	"I am America . . ." "African American World," PBS.org, http://www.pbs.org/wnet/aaworld/profiles/who.html.
p. 40,	"The conditions for . . ." Carson, *Civil Rights Chronicle*, 303.
p. 41,	"I have never . . ." Taylor Branch, *At Canaan's Edge* (New York: Simon & Schuster, 2006), 511.
p. 44,	"we will wear . . ." Mary Elizabeth King, *Mahatma Gandhi and Martin Luther King* (UNESCO Publishing, 1999), 221.
p. 44,	"'Black power' not . . ." "Civil Rights: Ahead of Its Time," *Time*, September 30, 1966, http://www.time.com/time/magazine/article/0,9171,836425-2,00.html.
p. 44,	"based upon the . . ." Ibid.
p. 44,	"Anyone leading a . . ." Martin Luther King Jr., *Where Do We Go From Here: Chaos or Community?* (Boston: Beacon Press, 2010), 58.
p. 44,	"I guess I . . ." Ibid., 26.

CHAPTER 4: BLACK MILITANCY

p. 47,	"All right, brothers . . ." Bobby Seale, *Seize the Time* (Baltimore: Black Classic Press, 1991), 155.
p. 48,	"Look at Reagan . . ." Ibid.
p. 48,	"Man they were . . ." Ibid., 157.

p. 48,	"I looked at . . ." Ibid., 159.
p. 48,	"The Black Panther . . ." Philip Sheldon Foner and Clayborne Carson, *The Black Panthers Speak* (Cambridge, Mass.: Da Capo Press, 2002), 40.
p. 49,	"The enslavement of . . ." Seale, *Seize the Time*, 162.
p. 50,	"1. We want freedom . . ." "History of the Black Panther Party," Stanford University, http://www.stanford.edu/group/blackpanthers/history.shtml.
p. 51,	"we will not . . ." Ibid.
p. 51,	"because they have . . ." Ibid.
p. 51,	"We believe that . . ." Ibid.
pp. 52-53,	"As I suffered . . ." Huey P. Newton, *Revolutionary Suicide* (New York: Harcourt Brace Jovanovich, 1973), 20.
p. 53,	"to carry their . . ." Ibid., 110.
p. 54,	"Inside of most . . ." Hampton and Fayer, *Voices of Freedom*, 376.
p. 54,	"Television showed pictures . . ." Ibid., 387.
p. 56,	"The city's vast . . ." "Newark," Riots—1967, http://www.67riots.rutgers.edu/n_index.htm.
p. 57,	"I see all . . ." "The Cambridge Riots of 1963 and 1967," Teaching American History, http://teachingamericanhistorymd.net/000001/000000/000033/html/t33.html.
p. 58,	"It shall now . . ." Carson, *Civil Rights Chronicle*, 328.
p. 58,	"This is our . . ." "Two Societies, Separate and Unequal, 1968," PBS.org, http://www.pbs.org/wgbh/amex/eyesontheprize/sources/ps_detroit.html.
p. 59,	"The most significant . . ." Carson, *Civil Rights Chronicle*, 329.
p. 59,	"Systematically all the . . ." "DRUM: Vanguard of the Black Revolution," libcom.org, http://libcom.org/library/drum-vanguard-black-revolution.
p. 60,	"Well, well, well . . ." "People v. Newton," CVN Law School, http://www.audiocasefiles.com/acf_cases/8631-people-v-newton.
p. 60,	"Free Huey! Off . . ." Carson, *Civil Rights Chronicle*, 353.
p. 62,	"It delighted me . . ." Lynn A. Higgins and Brenda R. Silver, *Rape and Representation* (New York: Columbia University Press, 1993), 86.
p. 62,	"If Eldridge Cleaver . . ." "'He was a symbol': Eldridge Cleaver Dies at 62," CNN.com, May 1, 1998, http://www.cnn.com/US/9805/01/cleaver.late.obit.
p. 62,	"Support White Power . . ." Carson, *Civil Rights Chronicle*, 337.
p. 63,	"to guarantee liberties . . ." Martin Luther King Jr., *A Testament of Hope* (New York: HarperCollins, 1990), 233.
p. 63,	"The black man . . ." Stewart Kellerman, "Soul Session in Vietnam," *United Press International*, April 25, 1971, http://100years.upi.com/sta_1971-04-25.html.
p. 63,	"blatant racist . . ." Seale, *Seize the Time*, 338.
p. 63,	"Though your brother's . . ." "Crosby Stills Nash Young—Chicago," Lyrics Download, http://www.lyricsdownload.com/crosby-stills-nash-young-chicago-lyrics.html.
p. 65,	"People thought the . . ." "Two Raised Fists," International Medalist Association, http://www.internationalmedalist.org/two_raised_fists.htm.
p. 65,	"Time is running . . ." Ronald P. Salzberger and Mary Turck, *Reparations for Slavery* (Lanham, Md.: Rowman & Littlefield, 2004), 70.
pp. 65-66,	"a research skills . . ." Ibid., 71.
p. 66,	"Oh, my God . . ." Carson, *Civil Rights Chronicle*, 359.

CHAPTER 5: "I'M BLACK AND I'M PROUD"

p. 69,   "Mildred, you are . . ." Carson, *Civil Rights Chronicle*, 356.

p. 70,   "You can plainly . . ." Ibid., 47.

p. 70,   "If dogs had . . ." Charlie Vascellaro, *Hank Aaron* (Santa Barbara, Calif.: Greenwood Publishing Group, 2005), 17.

pp. 70-71,   "The most insidious . . ." "Stokely Carmichael," University of Washington, http://courses.washington.edu/spcmu/carmichael/transcript.htm.

p. 72,   "Go home. . ." Jack Canfield, et al., *Chicken Soup for the African American Soul* (Deerfield Beach, Fla.: HCI, 2004), 178.

p. 72,   "a consummate moment . . ." Eric Wilson, "Naomi Sims, 61, Pioneering Cover Girl, Is Dead," *New York Times*, August 3, 2009, http://www.nytimes.com/2009/08/04/fashion/04sims.html.

p. 72,   "adopted a Blacker-than-thou . . ." Alvin F. Poussaint, "From Self-Doubt to 'Black Is Beautiful,'" *Ebony*, November 1985, 114.

p. 74,   "Say it loud . . ." "Say It Loud—I'm Black and I'm Proud," Songfacts, http://www.songfacts.com/detail.php?id=10289.

p. 74,   "We wanted to . . ." Hugh Moffett, "U.S. of. A.: Where Are You?" *Life*, April 19, 1968, 98.

p. 75,   "Hoppin' John (black-eyed . . ." "Red, Black & Greens: The Politics of Soul Food in the 1960s," Black Vegetarians, http://www.blackvegetarians.org/features/httpwww.blackvegetarians.orgfeaturesredblackgreens.htm.

p. 76,   "I think what . . ." Kevin Chappell, "Rock and Roll," *Ebony*, July 2001, 146.

p. 76,   "Aretha's music makes . . ." "Lady Soul Singing It Like It Is," *Time*, June 28, 1968, http://www.time.com/time/magazine/article/0,9171,841340-2,00.html.

p. 77,   "It's time that . . ." Peniel E. Joseph, *The Black Power Movement* (Boca Raton, Fla.: CRC Press, 2006), 229–230.

p. 78,   "black-oriented neighborhood schools . . ." "Black Power," Amistad Digital Resource, http://www.amistadresource.org/civil_rights_era/black_power.html.

p. 79,   "At the moment . . ." Joanne Morreale, *Critiquing the Sitcom* (Syracuse: Syracuse University Press, 2003), 138.

p. 80,   "aesthetic and spiritual . . ." aalbc.com, http://aalbc.com/authors/blackartsmovement.htm.

p. 80,   "Blacks gave the . . ." Ibid.

p. 81,   "Sisters . . . did not . . ." "But Some of Us Are Brave," Massachusetts Institute of Technology, http://web.mit.edu/activities/thistle/v9/9.01/6blackf.html.

pp. 81-82,   "What made 'The . . ." Frank Rich, "'The Wiz' Back on Broadway," *New York Times*, May 25, 1984, http://theater.nytimes.com/mem/theater/treview.html?id=1077011432896&html_title=&tols_title=&byline=&fid=NONE.

CHAPTER 6: BACKLASH AND PROGRESS

p. 85,   "You think I . . ." Hampton and Fayer, *Voices of Freedom*, 467.

p. 86,   "Now there is . . ." Henry J. Perkinson, *Getting Better* (Piscataway, N.J.: Transaction Publishers, 1996), 62.

p. 86,   "stand up on . . ." Ibid.

p. 87,	"forgotten majority—the . . ." Charles Lincoln Van Doren and Robert McHenry, eds., *Webster's Guide to American History* (Springfield, Mass.: G. & C. Merriam Co., 1971), 627.
p. 88,	"expose, disrupt, misdirect . . ." Hampton and Fayer, *Voices of Freedom*, 511-512.
p. 89,	"the greatest threat . . ." Ibid.
p. 89,	"In all, of . . ." Ibid.
p. 90,	"We wholeheartedly commend . . ." Frankie Y. Bailey and Steven M. Chermak, *Famous American Crimes and Trials: 1960-1980* (Santa Barbara, Calif.: Praeger, 2004), 90.
p. 90,	"It's like the . . ." Hampton and Fayer, *Voices of Freedom*, 514.
p. 91,	"take up arms . . ." "Former Black Liberation Army Members Arrested," Uprising, February 6, 2007, http://uprisingradio.org/home/?p=1194.
p. 94	"Black politics demands . . ." "The National Black Political Convention (1972)," PBS.org, http://www.pbs.org/wgbh/amex/eyesontheprize/milestones/m13_nbpc.html.
p. 95,	"White students who . . ." Jeffrey Ogbonna Green Ogbar, *Black Power* (Baltimore: Johns Hopkins University Press, 2005), 138.
p. 95,	"The fights, short . . ." Ibid., 139.
p. 99,	"There were lots . . ." "A Passion for Action," *BBC News*, August 21, 2003, http://news.bbc.co.uk/2/hi/americas/3150491.stm.

CHAPTER 7: BLACK POWER TODAY

p. 102,	"health care gap . . ." Herb Boyd and Todd Burroughs, *Civil Rights: Yesterday & Today* (Lincolnwood, Ill.: Publications International, 2010), 119.
p. 103,	"It's totally separate . . ." Kari Lydersen, "Boycott Underscores Disparities in Schools," *Washington Post*, September 5, 2008, http://www.washingtonpost.com/wp-dyn/content/article/2008/09/04/AR2008090403398.html.
p. 105,	"one in three . . ." "About Us," The Sentencing Project, http://www.sentencingproject.org/template/page.cfm?id=2.
pp. 105-106,	"I'm talking about . . ." Michael Eric Dyson, *Is Bill Cosby Right?* (New York: Basic Civitas Books, 2006), 59.
p. 106,	"It's cursing and . . ." Ibid., xiii.
p. 106,	"Dyson swings back . . ." Keith A. Owens, "Dyson Disses Cosby Cause," *Metro Times*, http://www.metrotimes.com/editorial/story.asp?id=7635.
p. 106,	"It's not good . . ." Lynn Sweet, "Obama Tells Blacks: Shape Up," *Chicago Sun-Times*, February 29, 2008, http://www.suntimes.com/news/sweet/819177,CST-NWS-sweet29.article.
p. 109,	"a unique, holistic . . ." "The HCZ Project," Harlem Children's Zone, http://www.hcz.org/about-us/the-hcz-project.
p. 109,	"Education is still . . ." Boyd and Burroughs, *Civil Rights: Yesterday & Today*, 187.

BIBLIOGRAPHY

aalbc.com. http://aalbc.com/authors/blackartsmovement.htm.

"About Us." The Sentencing Project. http://www.sentencingproject.org/template/page. cfm?id=2.

Bailey, Frankie Y., and Steven M. Chermak. *Famous American Crimes and Trials: 1960–1980*. Santa Barbara, Calif.: Praeger, 2004.

"African American World." PBS.org. http://www.pbs.org/wnet/aaworld/profiles/who.html.

Baldwin, James. *The Price of the Ticket*. New York: Macmillan, 1985.

"Black Power." Amistad Digital Resource. http://www.amistadresource.org/civil_rights_era/black_power.html.

Boyd, Herb, and Todd Burroughs. *Civil Rights: Yesterday & Today*. Lincolnwood, Ill.: Publications International, 2010.

Branch, Taylor. *At Canaan's Edge*. New York: Simon & Schuster, 2006.

"Brown v. Board of Education, 347 U.S. 483 (1954)." The National Center for Public Policy Research. http://www.nationalcenter.org/brown.html.

"But Some of Us Are Brave." Massachusetts Institute of Technology. http://web.mit.edu/activities/thistle/v9/9.01/6blackf.html.

"The Cambridge Riots of 1963 and 1967." Teaching American History. http://teachingamericanhistorymd.net/000001/000000/000033/html/t33.html.

Canfield, Jack, et al. *Chicken Soup for the African American Soul*. Deerfield Beach, Fla.: HCI, 2004.

Carson, Clayborne, primary consultant. *Civil Rights Chronicle*. Lincolnwood, Ill.: Legacy Publishing, 2003.

Chappell, Kevin. "Rock and Roll." *Ebony*, July 2001.

"Civil Rights: Ahead of Its Time." *Time*, September 30, 1966. http://www.time.com/time/magazine/article/0,9171,836425-2,00.html.

"Crosby Stills Nash Young—Chicago." Lyrics Download. http://www.lyricsdownload.com/crosby-stills-nash-young-chicago-lyrics.html.

"Deborah Rand," Civil Rights Movement Veterans. http://www.crmvet.org/vet/randd.htm.

"DRUM: Vanguard of the Black Revolution." libcom.org. http://libcom.org/library/drum-vanguard-black-revolution.

Dyson, Michael Eric. *Is Bill Cosby Right?* New York: Basic Civitas Books, 2006.

"A ESC Tribute to Malcolm X." Ethnic Student Center. http://esc.as.wwu.edu/x/quotes.html.

Foner, Philip Sheldon, and Clayborne Carson. *The Black Panthers Speak*. Cambridge, Mass.: Da Capo Press, 2002.

"Former Black Liberation Army Members Arrested." Uprising, February 6, 2007. http://uprisingradio.org/home/?p=1194.

Gottheimer, Josh. *Ripples of Hope: Great American Civil Rights Speeches*. New York: Basic Civitas Books, 2004.

Hamilton, Charles J., Jr. "SNCC: Brass Tacks." The *Harvard Crimson*. http://www.thecrimson.com/article/1967/5/4/sncc-pat-a-student-non-violent-coordinating.

Hampton, Henry, and Steve Fayer. *Voices of Freedom*. New York: Bantam Books, 1990.

"The HCZ Project." Harlem Children's Zone. http://www.hcz.org/about-us/the-hcz-project.

"'He Was a Symbol': Eldridge Cleaver Dies at 62." CNN.com. http://www.cnn.com/US/9805/01/cleaver.late.obit.

Higgins, Lynn A., and Brenda R. Silver. *Rape and Representation*. New York: Columbia University Press, 1993.

"History of the Black Panther Party." Stanford University. http://www.stanford.edu/group/blackpanthers/history.shtml.

Joseph, Peniel E. *The Black Power Movement*. Boca Raton, Fla.: CRC Press, 2006.

"Kareem Abdul-Jabbar." Emmett Till Murder. http://www.emmetttillmurder.com/Jabbar.htm.

Kaufman, Michael T. "Stokely Carmichael, Rights Leader Who Coined 'Black Power,' Dies at 57." *New York Times*, November 16, 1998. http://www.nytimes.com/1998/11/16/us/stokely-carmichael-rights-leader-who-coined-black-power-dies-at-57.html.

Kellerman, Stewart. "Soul Session in Vietnam." *United Press International*, April 25, 1971. http://100years.upi.com/sta_1971-04-25.html.

King, Martin Luther, Jr. *A Testament of Hope*. New York: HarperCollins, 1991.

_____. *Where Do We Go From Here: Chaos or Community?* Boston: Beacon Press, 2010.

King, Mary Elizabeth. *Mahatma Gandhi and Martin Luther King*. Paris: UNESCO Publishing, 1999.

"Lady Soul Singing It Like It Is." *Time*, June 28, 1968. http://www.time.com/time/magazine/article/0,9171,841340-2,00.html.

Lydersen, Kari. "Boycott Underscores Disparities in Schools." *Washington Post*, September 5, 2008. http://www.washingtonpost.com/wp-dyn/content/article/2008/09/04/AR2008090403398.html.

"Malcolm X Quotes." Thinkexist.com. http://thinkexist.com/quotation/be_peaceful-be_courteous-obey_the_law-respect/250988.html.

"Malcolm X Quotes." Thinkexist.com. http://thinkexist.com/quotation/nobody_can_give_you_freedom-nobody_can_give_you/251191.html.

"Martin Luther King, Jr./'I Have a Dream.'" American Rhetoric: Top 100 Speeches. http://www.americanrhetoric.com/speeches/mlkihaveadream.htm.

Moffett, Hugh. "U.S. of. A.: Where Are You?" *Life*, April 19, 1968.

Morreale, Joanne. *Critiquing the Sitcom*. Syracuse: Syracuse University Press, 2003.

"Mukasa Willie Ricks and the Voting Rights Act of 1965." Associated Content. http://www.associatedcontent.com/article/1208593/mukasa_willie_ricks_and_the_voting_pg2.html?cat=37.

Mulligan, Therese. *Bernie Boston*. Rochester, N.Y.: RIT Cary Graphic Arts Press, 2006.

"Nation of Islam." Allaahuakbar.net. http://www.allaahuakbar.net/nation/nation_of_islam.htm.

"The National Black Political Convention 1972." PBS.org. http://www.pbs.org/wgbh/amex/eyesontheprize/milestones/m13_nbpc.html.

"Newark." Riots—1967. http://www.67riots.rutgers.edu/n_index.htm.

Newton, Huey P. *Revolutionary Suicide*. New York: Harcourt Brace Jovanovich, 1973.

_____. Newton, Huey P., et al. *The Huey P. Newton Reader*. New York: Seven Stories Press, 2002.

"Nonviolence Quotes." BrainyQuote. http://www.brainyquote.com/quotes/keywords/nonviolence.html.

Ogbar, Jeffrey Ogbonna Green. *Black Power*. Baltimore: Johns Hopkins University Press, 2005.

"Our History." SCLC. http://sclcnational.org/core/item/page.aspx?s=25461.0.12.2607.

Owens, Keith A. "Dyson Disses Cosby Cause." *Metro Times*. http://www.metrotimes.com/editorial/story.asp?id=7635.

Parks, Gordon. "Whip of Black Power." *Life*, May 19, 1967.

"A Passion for Action." *BBC News*, August 21, 2003. http://news.bbc.co.uk/2/hi/americas/3150491.stm.

"People v. Newton." CVN Law School. http://www.audiocasefiles.com/acf_cases/8631-people-v-newton.

Perkinson, Henry J. *Getting Better*. Piscataway, N.J.: Transaction Publishers, 1996.

Poussaint, Alvin F. "From Self-Doubt to 'Black Is Beautiful.'" *Ebony*, November 1985.

"Quotations." malcolm-x.org. http://www.malcolm-x.org/quotes.htm.

"Red, Black & Greens: The Politics of Soul Food in the 1960s." *Black Vegetarians*. http://www.blackvegetarians.org/features/httpwww.blackvegetarians.orgfeaturesredblackgreens.htm.

Rich, Frank. "'The Wiz' Back on Broadway." *New York Times*, May 25, 1984. http://theater.nytimes.com/mem/theater/treview.html?id=1077011432896&html_title=&tols_title=&byline=&fid=NONE.

Salzberger, Ronald P., and Mary Turck. *Reparations for Slavery*. Lanham, Md.: Rowman & Littlefield, 2004.

"Say It Loud—I'm Black and I'm Proud." Songfacts. http://www.songfacts.com/detail.php?id=10289.

Seale, Bobby. *Seize the Time*. Baltimore: Black Classic Press, 1991.

Sellers, Cleveland. *The River of No Return*. Jackson: University Press of Mississippi, 1990.

"Stokely Carmichael." University of Washington. http://courses.washington.edu/spcmu/carmichael/transcript.htm.

Sweet, Lynn. "Obama Tells Blacks: Shape Up." *Chicago Sun-Times*, February 29, 2008. http://www.suntimes.com/news/sweet/819177,CST-NWS-sweet29.article.

"Three Speeches from Frederick Douglass: Examples of His Passion, Logic and Power." FrederickDouglass.org. http://www.frederickdouglass.org/speeches.

"Two Raised Fists." International Medalist Association. http://www.internationalmedalist.org/two_raised_fists.htm.

"Two Societies, Separate and Unequal, 1968." PBS.org. http://www.pbs.org/wgbh/amex/eyesontheprize/sources/ps_detroit.html.

Van Doren, Charles Lincoln, and Robert McHenry, eds. *Webster's Guide to American History*. Springfield, Mass.: G. & C. Merriam Co., 1971.

Vascellaro, Charlie. *Hank Aaron*. Santa Barbara, Calif.: Greenwood Publishing Group, 2005.

"W. E. B. DuBois: Address to the Nation." http://www.wfu.edu/~zulick/341/niagara.html.

"What We Believe." The Nation of Islam. http://www.noi.org/muslim_program.htm.

Williams, Juan. *Eyes on the Prize*. New York: Penguin Books, 1987.

Wilson, Eric. "Naomi Sims, 61, Pioneering Cover Girl, Is Dead." *New York Times*, August 3, 2009. http://www.nytimes.com/2009/08/04/fashion/04sims.html.

WEB SITES

www.npr.org/templates/story/story.php?storyId=102691304

Read or listen to a six minute, thirteen second NPR interview with Peniel Joseph, a professor of African American history at Brandeis University, on "'Black Power!': Inside the Movement"on this site.

americanrhetoric.com/speeches/stokelycarmichaelblackpower.html

A 1966 speech delivered by Stokely Carmichael in October of that year at the University of California, at Berkeley, is available to read on this site. Or, you can listen to the speech on an mp3 player.

www.amistadresource.org/civil_rights_era/black_power.html

The Amistad Digital Resource for Teaching African American History at Columbia University has an article on the Black Power movement in its section on the civil rights era.

INDEX

PICTURE CREDITS